If It Hadn't Been For Grace

If It Hadn't Been For Grace

by

Esther Harkess

DIADEM BOOKS

For you created my inmost being;
you knit me together in my mother's womb.
I praise you because I am fearfully and wonderfully made;
your works are wonderful,
I know that full well.
My frame was not hidden from you
when I was made in the secret place,
when I was woven together in the depths of the earth.
Your eyes saw my unformed body;
all the days ordained for me were written in your book
before one of them came to be.
Psalm 139 vs 13-16 (NIV)

I dedicate this book to my parents Joe and Hilda, who so lovingly welcomed me into their hearts and home, surrounding me with the security of their constant love and care.

Mummy and Daddy's wedding

Table of Contents

PROLOGUE

AGED **ELEVEN**, my world exploded quietly as I learnt that Mummy and Daddy were not my biological parents.

I had been adopted.

Now there were two girls, identical in every way except one had loving parents, the other, a mother who had given her away. One girl moved on, the other stood still, in a fantasy world imagining who she might be.

It was the moment that has affected me then and now and in between, more than I will ever know.

At the age of sixty-five, I decided to stop imagining and find out about the other me.

1

The Quiet Explosion

THE QUIET EXPLOSION occurred during the summer of 1955. It turned out to be a momentous summer.

Towards the end of the previous year I and the rest of my school class sat the dreaded eleven plus examination or grading exam as we called it hoping to gain a place at grammar school in Alnwick, Northumberland. The system was either a straight pass or an interview. The interview took place at the grammar school and was virtually another exam. No one gained a straight pass that year but ten of us gained interviews of which only four passed, and I was not one of them. Mummy took this news very badly and as I sobbed, I remember it being Daddy that comforted me. I suppose it must have been extremely hard for Mummy, who had taught in that school for twenty years prior to her marriage to have a daughter that failed to make the grade.

Mummy already had misgivings about me having to travel to Alnwick by bus every day, a journey of approximately fourteen miles. Given these circumstances, my parents thought it would be good for me to have a boarding school education. Once this decision was finalised, my parents then told me that I would be going to a boarding school called Craigmount, at Minto, near Hawick in the Scottish borders. I cannot actually remember my parents going to look at the school but I suppose they must have done so before making such a monumental decision, financially and emotionally. I of course never gave these matters any consideration, as I was so excited at the prospect of all those midnight feasts, pillow fights, etc., that I had so often read about in books.

The excitement continued. The clothing list came in. Off we went to Edinburgh to the school outfitters. It was some list – one tweed coat; one summer coat; one blazer; one gabardine raincoat, all of which had their own hats with the school badge prominently displayed. A gym tunic, to be worn with square necked blouses; a kilt or dark green skirt, shirt blouses and a school tie; two pairs of outdoor shoes; two pairs of indoor shoes – the list went on and on. A large trunk was required and an overnight suitcase. Everything had to have name-tapes sewn on including my own bedlinen and towels.

I had very long thick hair, which I wore in plaits. After washing my hair, it took ages to dry. We didn't have a hair dryer, so sitting in front of the coal fire had to suffice and once my hair was dry, Mummy would brush it meticulously. It was during one of these hairdressing sessions that Mummy said that she had something to tell me. Apparently, my future headmistress had advised her to tell me this story before I went to boarding school.

Mummy went on to tell me that after she and Daddy married in 1940, they lived in a farmhouse near Eyemouth in Berwickshire. Naturally, they often went to visit Mummy's family in Northumberland. During one such journey, they had a car accident, something to do with an army roadblock. This accident resulted in Mummy having a miscarriage and losing the baby boy that she had been expecting. Mummy and Daddy were devastated. With hindsight, I think that Mummy nearly lost her life as this tragedy happened in winter and the doctor and nurse had to walk through deep snow to reach her.

In 1943 they moved back to North Sunderland / Seahouses in Northumberland to live in the semi-detached bungalow next door to my grandparents and Mummy's sister Auntie Lah. They really did want a family and decided to see if they could adopt a baby, preferably a baby girl. This resulted in Auntie Martin, a close friend of Mummy, advising them to go to an adoption agency that she knew of through a friend who had connections with it. My parent's application to adopt a baby girl was successful and the wait began for a suitable baby. During this waiting period on the 1st December 1943 my grandmother died. This was another sad time for the family but there was to be good news for them before too long.

The adoption agency contacted them asking if they would like to adopt a baby girl born on the 5th December. My parents were delighted with the news, consequently travelling to London on the 22nd February 1944 and returning home with me, their baby girl on the 23rd February. They called me Esther after Mummy's mother and gave me a second name, Elizabeth after Daddy's mother. Mummy, having been a teacher, was used to dealing with older children but had no experience with babies. Auntie Lah however, even though not having a family herself, was very used to helping with the babies of friends, and on my parents' arrival back home with me, she had said to Mummy, 'Give her to me our Hilda, you know nothing about them!'

Quite a story for an eleven year old to hear whilst having her hair brushed! My only reaction to this story was that one or two things now made sense. Firstly, the family joke that Mummy had tried to give me away as soon as she got me. On arriving at King's Cross station in London at the start of our journey home, Mummy was frightened to step onto the escalator with me in her arms. A very kind man asked Mummy if he could carry me for her and she readily agreed! Daddy couldn't help Mummy as he had the luggage and would also have had to manage my gas mask, a huge contraption as the whole baby was placed inside (it looks like a spaceman's helmet, I know as I still have it). I had never wondered why my parents should go to London for me; at my age then, children knew very little about the facts of life and as far as I was concerned, anybody might have gone to London to get their baby. A second strange memory that I had buried away in the recesses of my mind was hearing an elderly man who went to Chapel say to Daddy, 'It's amazing how like you she looks.'

I have only those few memories about my initial reaction to the news of my adoption. Probably this was because of me having a happy and secure childhood. There was no anger or feeling of rejection. However, on reflection, I know that my life changed that day and was never the same again. I had suddenly become, as it were, two different people, with two different mothers and had a sense of belonging nowhere.

2

Mother and Father

WITH HINDSIGHT, the previous eleven years had been idyllic as I grew up in the villages of North Sunderland and Seahouses, Northumberland. Both of my parents were Northumbrian but were not born in North Sunderland or Seahouses. They were very different in character but complemented each other very well. My father was gregarious and easy going, my mother private, gentle, but very determined.

My father Joseph was born and brought up by his parents George and Elizabeth, in Christon Bank, a small village north of Alnwick in Northumberland. George and Elizabeth had six children, two sons and four daughters. A known family in the area, they were instrumental in the building of the Methodist Chapel on land given to them by Sir Edward Grey of Fallodon who was at one time Foreign Secretary. The story is that everyone agreed that Grandfather should be the person to approach Sir Edward to ask for land on which to build the Chapel. This he did while his seven brothers held a prayer meeting. He returned with good news; the Chapel was built and was one of several that Grandfather preached in during his forty years of being a Methodist local preacher. The Chapel is still in use today with members of the family still worshipping there.

On leaving school, my father joined his brother in the undertaking and coach building business of their Uncle Hugh in Alnwick. At the outbreak of the First World War, he and his brother both joined up, serving in the Royal Flying Corp. My father had an exceptional singing voice, which was described to me quite recently as 'That wonderful Italian tenor voice' and he sang wherever he went. Being a committed Christian, he loved to sing gospel hymns and I still have his well-worn Redemption Hymnal, which went right through the war with him. He used to tell of how he sang in the barracks and of the ridicule that he was subjected to, when he knelt to pray each night before going to bed.

My mother, Hilda, was born in Wooler, a small market town that nestles at the foot of the Cheviot Hills. She was the younger daughter of John and Esther. Growing up in Wooler, she firstly went to the local Church of England school and later travelled daily by train to Alnwick, where she attended the Duchess School.

Like my father, my mother grew up going to the Methodist Chapel and her father was a local preacher too. With these strong Methodist connections, the paths of my father and mother inevitably crossed. One romantic story is of how my father would walk my mother to the station in Alnwick after school, and on one of these walks, he was feeding her strawberries en route!

After school my mother went to train as a teacher at Darlington Teacher Training College (until recently the town's Arts Centre), after which she taught on Tyneside for one year and then at North Sunderland / Seahouses. Her father's family were builders and monumental masons, their business being in Wooler. However, having started to build in North Sunderland and Seahouses, they also had a home there whilst my mother was at school. This meant that the family travelled regularly between their homes in Seahouses and Wooler. Consequently, my mother was no stranger to the villages of North Sunderland / Seahouses where she was to teach for twenty years.

As I have already mentioned my father singing, my mother was also gifted musically. Initially playing the violin but when training to be a teacher, she had three months of piano lessons. She was quite remarkable in her ability to hear a tune, write it down in tonic solfa (doh-reh-me) and then be able to go to the piano and harmonise it immediately.

After returning from the war my father and his brother bought their uncle's business when he died. Later they decided to sell it and go their separate ways. About this time and following the completion of my mother's teacher training, my father proposed marriage to her. He was rejected. My mother told him that she had a teaching career to pursue. At this stage, my father moved to Eyemouth, a fishing port on the Berwickshire coast just a few miles over the Scottish border where he opened a bakery business. Here my father continued to live and eventually he married someone else. This marriage ended when his wife died a few years later. When in Eyemouth he was a very active member and office bearer at the Methodist Chapel but also found time to be involved in local politics and served as a town councillor for a number of years, after a while becoming a Junior Baillie. Needless to say music and singing were still very much part of his life and he sang in the Berwick Choral Society and the Chapel choir. Later, he sang in the Seahouses Fishermen's Choir and often entertained his little daughter by singing stories to her. Two firm favourites were Hiawatha and the Pied Piper of Hamelin.

My mother meanwhile continued her teaching career in North Sunderland / Seahouses and ran the Christian Endeavour, an organisation for young people, also helping with a girls' bible class in Auntie Martin's home.

Obviously, my father was of the opinion that faint heart never won fair lady and once again proposed to my mother, apparently while she was digging daisies out of the lawn! After twenty years of teaching, she happily accepted and they were married in Seahouses Methodist Chapel in October 1940. After spending their honeymoon at The Romany House Hotel, Yetholm, in the Scottish Borders, their first home was the farmhouse near Eyemouth. Later they moved to North Sunderland / Seahouses, next door to my Wooler grandparents and aunt. Having sold his bakery business my father had become a bee farmer and supplied stores such as Fortnum and Mason in London and Dymock and Howden in Edinburgh, so the bees were relocated too!

3

Home and Village

NORTH SUNDERLAND was the original village. 'Sunder', meaning south, was the land south of Bamburgh, the capital of Northumbria. When another Sunderland appeared in County Durham, a distinguishing prefix was required. Seahouses came into being in the 18th century when the local fishermen built their houses near the harbour. However, the harbour at Seahouses was still known as North Sunderland Harbour, remaining that way until fairly recently. In the late 1800's the railway arrived linking Seahouses and North Sunderland to the main east coast line at Chathill. The original owners were the North Sunderland Railway Company and then it became part of the London North Eastern Railway. There were stations at both North Sunderland and Seahouses and the train was known locally as 'The Tanky.' Sadly, the line closed in 1951.

Our home was a lovely detached house built by my Wooler grandfather, using stone of a reddish colour from a local quarry, the same stone that was used to build Auntie Martin's home and the Methodist Chapel (again built by my Wooler grandfather). Our home 'Romany' was called after the hotel where my parents spent their honeymoon. This enhanced my father's romantic idea that if you went far enough back in his family there would be a gipsy connection. There is no proof of this but it is highly probable on my mother's side! Wooler Grandfather built 'Romany' for his own family home but my grandmother refused to move preferring to stay in the semi-detached bungalow called 'West Rays',so called because the main public rooms faced west. 'West Rays' and the adjoining bungalow where we lived from 1943—May 1945 were built of a lovely mellow coloured stone, rather like that found in the Cotswolds.

Wooler grandparents in West Rays garden

'Romany' had nooks and crannies but grandfather always said he would have built a better house had he not used an architect. The house was at one time let to our local doctor; he required a surgery so this and a waiting room were added onto the washhouse and coalhouse. These changes led to us having four external doors, which was highly convenient for me as a child, having four escape routes to Auntie Lah at 'West Rays' when I had been naughty!

Our garden was large with a small copse of sycamore trees at the bottom which we called 'The Plantation'. The first flowers to bloom were clumps of snowdrops planted beside the graves of various pets, all having their own wooden plaques made by my father and inscribed by my mother. However, the crowning glory in 'The Plantation' was the carpet of bluebells during the month of May. It was in 'The plantation' that I spent many happy times on my swing, which hung from a branch of one of the sycamore trees.

To one side of 'The Plantation' a grassy path ran along the bottom of the next door garden and ended at 'West Rays'. Another large garden beckoned me but it was different from ours as it was open and not shaded by trees. The lawn was a full sized tennis court and my mother used to boast that prior to her marriage she cut it with a hand mower and then played on it. 'West Rays' lawn and garden conjures up memories of playing clock golf, making daisy chains and watching pied wagtails with their tails bobbing up and down as they searched for food. Likewise, thrushes having found their next meal would smash the unfortunate snail on the driveway.

Mummy loved birds and in the garden or when walking in the farm lane at the back of the houses she taught me to recognise their songs. 'A little bit of bread and no cheese' from the yellow hammers and the glorious song of the skylarks as they soared heavenwards, eventually becoming tiny specks in the sky. At Romany, we had a tame chaffinch called Pinkie, so named because of the pink, pink sound of its call. Pinkie would tap his beak on the dining room window; we would open it and he would hop inside where a dish of seed awaited him. The open porch at the front of the house saw swallows return year after year and Mummy would never allow the washing of the step until they had gone! With this love of birds, cats were definitely not welcome and Mummy encouraged all dogs to chase them off the premises. All the dogs needed to hear was the blackbirds alarm call, and they were off in search of the feline intruder.

With Daddy being a bee farmer our garden buzzed with the sound of bees; my parents would tell me not to go near the beehives but curiosity got the better of me and I ended up having many stings.

Being a man who liked a joke, my father after purchasing a stone rabbit to place in the garden summoned the local rabbit catcher who failed to be amused but forgave my father and his sense of humour!

Romany and garden

Romany front door

4

Relatives in Abundance

W ITH US MOVING into 'Romany' and my grandfather remarrying about the same time, Auntie Lah was left alone in 'West Rays' and our bungalow was let to an older couple called Young. Mr Young had been the gardener at Shoreston Hall just outside the village. The rent for the bungalow was low in exchange for Mr Young being the gardener at 'West Rays'. They were very much grandparent figures to me and I ended up calling them Uncle Arthur and Auntie Young. I can still remember the smell of cooking bacon wafting out from their kitchen as I ran past going to see Nanny, that being what I called Auntie Lah.

Apparently I could not say Auntie when very small so Auntie Lah became Nanny, although for a while I had called her Bang, Bang, because of her habit of banging the back door when she left! I was her only niece but she was Auntie Lah (short for Annzillah) to numerous other children but to me she was my much loved and adored Nanny. She and Mummy (as I always called my mother) were very close in age and as sisters but very different in many ways and I being an extremely fortunate little girl had the best of both worlds. From now on, I will refer to Nanny as Auntie Lah as that is how I am used to referring to her within the family. My father I called Daddy and that is how I will refer to him.

Down the road towards Seahouses just past the school, there was a small bungalow where Uncle Bobby and Auntie Bessie lived. Uncle Bobby was the widower of Auntie Sarah, my Wooler Grandmother's sister. Auntie Bessie was Uncle Bobby's sister who kept house for him. We would visit them after Chapel on Sunday evenings and a dish of sweets was always on the table for us to enjoy, the selection being either Black bullets, Berwick cockles or Pan drops.

Further down the road lived a cousin of Daddy's who was also a close friend of Auntie Lah; her name was Auntie Cissie and she was very involved in my childhood. I still find myself doing things that Auntie Lah and Auntie Cissie taught me such as in cooking (I always use Auntie Cissie's marmalade recipe), homemaking and flower arranging, and as I got older Auntie Cissie and I would go on long walks together.

Next door but one to Auntie Cissie lived Mummy's close friend Auntie Martin who was one of my Godmothers and she was a character. Her father had been Archdeacon of Lindisfarne and the family had an aristocratic background traced back to one of Wellington's generals who had fought at the battle of Waterloo. She owned a large walled garden at the North Sunderland end of the village where she grew vegetables and soft fruit. It was wonderful to pick and sometimes eat red and white currants all growing against the walls and blackcurrants and gooseberries off the bushes. A local greengrocer then sold the produce with the money going to support missionaries.

Auntie Martin had Bunsy, a white rabbit, who sat on the hearth keeping warm by the fire and Punch, the tortoise, who hibernated in one of the spare bedrooms. On winter Sundays, Auntie Martin would call in to Romany and collect a baked potato on her way home from St Paul's C/E, North Sunderland. The potatoes baked in our Aga-type cooker while we were at Chapel. This was normal Sunday lunch fare along with cold meat. Mummy cooked the 'Sunday' roast on a Monday when Auntie Martin would also join us. When very small I was quite reluctant to eat my dinner and Auntie Martin would coax me by telling me stories about Johnny and his boat. Johnny was a boatman figure in a picture, which hung in our dining room. I am glad to say that Johnny is still with me to remind me of those occasions.

Now we retrace our steps back up the main road into North Sunderland passing the school on the right with 'Romany' and 'West Rays' on the left. A littleway further on was the police station, next to which was one of the old village water pumps. Carrying on, we would then arrive at a small shop owned by Auntie Annie, the wife of Uncle Dick, another cousin of Daddy. Auntie Annie's shop never changed at all. I remember the large block of butter from which she would cut off and weigh the required amount, carefully wrapping it up in greaseproof paper. Choosing which biscuits we were to have was a special treat. Gipsy Creams weighed and put in a paper bag were a favourite and it was there that we bought fizzy drinks, returning the bottles when empty and collecting the money on them. Recycling is nothing new!

Uncle Dick and Auntie Annie were very much part of Sundays too. I sat beside them every Sunday evening from the time I was old enough to attend evening services at Chapel. Both my parents and Auntie Cissie were in the choir and Auntie Lah would be playing the organ. I can remember as a little girl looking around the congregation and choir and deciding which ladies' hat I liked best!

The last person in my close extended family located in the village was Auntie 'B', officially known as Miss Brundell or AJB by those she had taught at the Duchess School in Alnwick including Mummy and Auntie Lah. The Brundell family had also been next-door neighbours of my grandparents in Wooler when Mummy and Auntie Lah were very small, so they knew each other very well. On retiring Auntie 'B' had no home of her own as she had always lived in lodgings near the school. As Auntie Lah was alone in the family home in North

Sunderland, my grandfather having relocated back to Wooler following his remarraige, it seemed a good idea for her to offer Auntie 'B' a home. Therefore, Auntie 'B' became part of the family and along with Auntie Young from next door provided a good source of babysitting/ childminding for my parents. Auntie 'B' also spent several weeks each year with a cousin in York and I really looked forward to her return from those holidays as she always brought me Terry's Neapolitan chocolates!

Main Street Seahouses
The different houses in the above picture are: 1) West Rays;
2) My first home; 3) Romany; 4) Primary school.

During my early childhood Auntie Mabel, a friend of Mummy who taught French in a London school, often came to stay for the summer holidays. She would come and stay with Auntie Lah at 'West Rays' as her family had been friends of my grandparents. Sometimes her parents came too and as they fondly called Mummy their other daughter, I followed on by calling them Gran and Pappa as did their three grandsons. Papa was a retired Methodist minister with pure white hair and a long beard. Because of his appearance, people would sometimes refer to him as 'The Apostle'. Gran was tiny, and was always busy knitting and crocheting and would call me 'ducky'. The middle grandson was just slightly older than me and would sometimes come with Auntie Mabel without the rest of his family. I suppose this was the nearest I got to having a cousin of about the same age as me. My real cousins, the children of Daddy's brother and sister, were old enough to be my parents. This adopted cousin and I were sometimes joined by a daughter of one of Daddy's cousins and we had great fun with trips to the beach and playing in the gardens. I remember having an imaginary chemist's shop with him and making all kinds of brews and potions, which we tried to sell to our adult customers. Not a surprising pretence for one destined to become a dentist and the other a nurse. I had a vivid imagination and had my own chemist shops, when I was not at all interested in medicine, but in toiletries and make up. Rose petals can become wonderful colour swatches for powder, lipstick and nail varnish!

Happy days with Auntie Mabel

5

Idyllic Childhood

SOME PEOPLE say that they cannot remember anything prior to school but I certainly can. Mummy kept a sweetie tin in one of the kitchen cupboards; 'the rosy tin', so named because of the rosebud design. I can remember sitting in my pushchair about to go for a walk and Mummy giving me jelly babies or some other favourite out of the 'rosy tin.' That same cupboard housed the unmarked salt and sugar jars. My daily cod liver oil was on a spoonful of sugar. The inevitable happened. Salt took the place of the sugar, UGH! It certainly did not help the medicine go down! Another memory is of having breakfast in the kitchen, when Kym, the Yorkshire terrier, arrived from Auntie Lah's house and was saying good morning in a doggy sort of way to Rory, our black Cocker Spaniel. Rory died well before I started school. The winter of 1947 when I was very definitely pre-school, was terrible. I remember us walking to the top of North Sunderland to see where the snowplough had cut through a very high drift and there being walls of snow on either side of the road. Then retracing our steps and walking down to Seahouses in the middle of the road on the deeply rutted snow. Being so near the sea this was highly unusual and I cannot remember it ever being like that again.

After the death of both Rory and Kym our next dog was Mickie, a Yorkshire terrier, who was lovely except for definitely being a one-man or in this case a one-woman dog, the woman being Mummy. Unfortunately, several people, including me, experienced a canine bite; however, when the baker left the gate open poor Mickie ventured out and was run over on the road outside the house. Enter Mickie the second, whose nature was so different and he became a much-loved pet for sixteen years. He was so docile that I could dress him up and wheel him around in my doll's pram, which is something that I also did with one of our bantams, although not the dressing up bit! We had several bantams and I must say they kept us very well supplied with eggs, Mummy preserving any extra in a substance called waterglass enabling us to have a constant supply of eggs. One of my favourite breakfasts was an egg mixed up in a cup. The recipe being: take a lightly boiled egg and mix with small chunks of bread, add a good dollop of butter, season and enjoy.

I love egg sandwiches and my childhood memories of those are of coming down to the dining room in my dressing gown when my parents were entertaining the local clergy. This was after the annual general meeting of the local branch of The British and Foreign Bible Society of which Mummy was both secretary and treasurer. Egg sandwiches were always on the menu.

Christmas was very special. I loved all the preparations especially writing a letter to Father Christmas, which I posted up the chimney. That postal service was so efficient! There was an immense sense of wonder when waking up on Christmas morning and finding that Father Christmas had been kind, sometimes leaving what I had requested or sometimes surprises. We always had a Christmas tree decorated with tinsel, decorations of different kinds, some made by Mummy and lights acquired by my grandfather – small bulbs painted in varying colours. I also remember telling the local greengrocer that he had to supply me with a Christmas tree for the rest of my life. The wise man did indicate that this might not be possible.

Grandfather and his second wife, who I called Auntie Flossie, would be staying at 'West Rays' and we would all go to the Christmas morning service at Chapel. On returning home

Christmas dinner was always at 'Romany' and we feasted on a locally bred turkey along with all the trimmings. Christmas pudding made by Auntie Lah was to follow served with her special type of sauce made with water! As I often seemed to be ill at Christmas with flu or something of that nature, dinner did not matter very much to me but I did love the time after dinner when all the adults received their gifts. These were waiting under the Christmas tree along with one or two small items that Mummy had kept aside for me. Father Christmas, (Daddy dressed up in a Father Christmas mask complete with beard) did an excellent job of distributing the various gifts. The tradition of receiving gifts after lunch continues with my own family up to the present day.

Later in the day, we went to 'West Rays' for Christmas tea after which we would play games. On Boxing Day, we did everything in reverse, taking the cold turkey to 'West Rays' for lunch and afterwards having tea at 'Romany' when we would sample Mummy's Christmas cake. Mummy had never really cooked until she married at the age of 41 and she had to cope with our unreliable cooker whose temperature could suddenly drop with a change of wind direction so Christmas cakes could be a challenge, one which she mostly overcame.

Christmas presents varied over the years, Daddy making a number of them. One year I received a doll's cot made by him,containing a doll called Violet which had belonged to Mummy and been beautifully dressed in clothes made by Auntie Lah who not only made beautiful dresses for dolls but also for me. Another year Daddy surpassed himself when he produced 'We Folks Villa', a doll's house complete with electric light (run off batteries), which was a near replica of 'Romany'. Auntie Lah had once again been busy, making curtains and other furnishings for the new property.

6

The Best Decision

ALTHOUGH AN ONLY CHILD I had plenty of friends. My best friend from pre-school and right through primary school was Joan who lived down the road in Seahouses. She was an only child too and we spent a lot of time together. However, I do remember at some point having imaginary brothers and sisters.

My formal education began in the September prior to my fifth birthday, when I started at North Sunderland County School, located slightly down the road but on the opposite side from Romany. We had the pleasure of having the playing fields opposite the house. This meant that it was often the case of leaving the house more or less when the school bell rang! However, during my first year at school I had to walk up the road to the parish church hall where the infant's class was located. I don't remember too much about this except at playtime; the milk had a horrible taste because of the crates containing the milk bottles standing outside in the sun.

I can honestly say that I enjoyed primary school. I loved nature study and will always remember the beautiful Indian Moon moths that we reared, as well as the stick insects. We studied all the usual subjects and I still have my primary school reports so know I was always near the top of the class. Once a week after school, I had a piano lesson, my teacher being the Church of England organist and I had other teachers at home!

Activities connected to the Methodist Chapel were very much part of my childhood. I went to Sunday school, taken there by Auntie Lah who taught in the senior Sunday school. The Methodist Church held annual scripture exams and I took part in these; if one passed there was a prize at the annual prize giving along with prizes for good attendance. Around the age of eight we were able to join the junior choir, which sang at Sunday morning services, the choir leaving just before the sermon when I would then go and sit with my parents. We always enjoyed the annual Sunday school picnic when several coaches would take us away for the day with parents and friends joining in. The Sunday school anniversary held in November was an amazing occasion. A platform was erected where the choir usually sat, enabling the congregation to see the children easily. Auntie Lah and other teachers were extremely professional in their planning of the programmes and it was one of the highlights of the year.

Another highlight during the course of the year at Chapel was the harvest thanksgiving. The Chapel was always beautifully decorated and the smell of flowers and fruit quite special. Mummy always gave a small basket full of our bantam's eggs. Nasturtiums picked from our garden were arranged at intervals along the front of the long trestle table bearing all the produce. The following evening we would congregate in the Sunday school room where the local auctioneer, a Chapel member, would sell the produce to the highest bidder and the bidding often became quite competitive and of course raised money for Chapel funds.

The Seahouses Fishermens choir were in great demand singing at many churches in the locality and others much further afield. Auntie Lah was the organist and Daddy sang in the choir in spite of him not being a fisherman; his solo or solos were always at the end of the programme and an encore was normally required. During March and August, an extremely popular event at Chapel was the Festival of the Sea. The fishermen decorated Chapel with fishing nets, model boats and other objects with connections to the sea and of course The Fishermen's choir sang.

Fishermen's choir with Auntie Lah at the organ

Attending the senior choir practice during the school holidays was something of a treat when I was small and I always stood on a chair next to Mummy. Even now when hearing some verses of scripture I find myself singing them in my head, having sung and heard them so often in anthems as a child.

In November 1953, when I was nine years old, we visited my grandfather in Wooler, when the Faith Mission was holding a series of meetings; in the evening there was a meeting for children to which I was taken by my parents. At the end of the meeting, the speaker asked if anyone wanted to ask Jesus into their heart and life to put up their hand. I knew that this was something I wanted to do but was too scared to put up my hand. However, when we returned home later that evening, I went to my bedroom and asked the Lord Jesus into my heart and life. Later I went downstairs and told Mummy what I had done, and she was overjoyed as was Daddy! I know that some people say that a child cannot possibly understand what they are doing. I certainly knew what I was doing. I knew the Bible said that only Jesus could forgive all the wrong things that I had done. That was why He died on the cross. I also knew that whoever acknowledges that they do wrong, in other words sin, and asks for His forgiveness, accepting Him as their saviour, they then have the assurance that when their earthly lives end or when Jesus comes again, they will go to be with Him in heaven. As I grew older I understood this in much greater depth and have never regretted making that decision when a small child. The Bible tells us in the book of Mark, chapter 10, verse 5, that Jesus says, 'I tell you the truth, anyone who will not receive the Kingdom of God like a little child, will never enter it.' This is so simple even a little child can understand what it means. Perhaps adults have a lot to learn from little children.

Later that month I was to experience the death of someone close to the family – Auntie Martin. People dying was not unheard of in our household as Daddy had returned to undertaking setting up his own business in the village, but Auntie Martin dying obviously had a large impact on our family. She had been so much part of it and to me it was like losing a grandmother.

Auntie Martin

7

Broadening Horizons

SEPTEMBER 1955 saw me embarking on my time at boarding school. Packing and unpacking became a very significant part of my life. We could have one large trunk and one small overnight case. All our possessions apart from what we needed for our first night of term went into the trunk with sports equipment such as hockey sticks and tennis racquets going separately. My parents took me by car as there was no suitable rail link and on that first day in September 1955 Auntie Lah came too. Our journey took us north, then southwest through the gently rolling countryside of the Borders, our final destination being in the county of Roxburghshire. En route we passed the Waterloo monument, a 150-foot tower situated on Peniel Heugh, a hill between Jedburgh and Hawick. This was to become a landmark on those school journeys, as when reaching this point in the journey I knew we were very close to school and on subsequent journeys, my heart sank. On we went, passing through Denholm, an attractive village dating back to the 17th century, with houses built around the village green. Beside Denholm is Ruberslaw Hill at approximately 1392 feet. Slightly to the north are the Minto Hills, Big Minto and Little Minto, not so high at around 912 feet. I did climb all of these hills at various times when at school. It was of course to Minto we were heading so we followed a minor road from Denholm, crossing the river Teviot and finally arriving at the school gates just before reaching Minto village.

Ready for boarding school

First journey to boarding school with Mummy, Daddy and Auntie Lah

The driveway wound round through lovely parkland before arriving at the front of the house, which was certainly very much larger than the one I had just left. The best description of the house is perhaps an inverted V-shape, the original being a central tower dating a long way back with the later addition of two wings. The stone-work terrace made an excellent stage and perfect setting for the performance of plays in the summer term. During the Second World War, the house was requisitioned, later being leased in 1952 to Craigmount Girls School. Craigmount, originally an Edinburgh school for boys, opened in 1874, then closed, reopening in 1884 as a boarding school for girls. In 1939 the school was evacuated to Scone Palace near Perth, relocating to Minto House in 1952.

Arrival at front door of boarding school

On arrival at school my parents and I were given a tour of the building ending at the dormitory that I was to share with six other girls. Thankfully, another girl was new and we soon made friends. My parents left. I was still extremely excited at the prospect of the new adventure that lay ahead. We unpacked our overnight cases, had supper and prepared for bed.

After breakfast on the first morning, we unpacked our trunks which were awaiting us in the library on the ground floor. We used the tray inside our trunks to carry the contents up to our dormitory, a long climb if you were on the top floor. Then to the basement where the boot room was located; here outerwear was deposited along with wellingtons, hockey boots, etc. The first and last day of term saw us having a reasonably good keep fit session!

Our day started with the rising bell at 7am and for those who wished, there was Scripture Union at 7.40am in the drawing room. This was the only time we entered that room except when sitting a music exam! One of the 5th or 6th years led Scripture Union by reading the bible portion for that day. We were very fortunate in having a Christian headmistress and other members of the teaching staff who also took part. I must confess I did not always get up in time!

Breakfast was at 8am and we congregated in the basement corridors before meals, lining up in our different houses. I was in Holmwood, but later when the names were changed, St Columba's became my house.

The dining room was still resplendent with the Minto family portraits. Long tables went down each side of the room and across both ends with the staff table in the centre. We moved seats every day and those at the end of the table cleared the dishes. One of the end tables was the dishes table where those who were on dishes duty sat; these girls, one from each form, served the other tables and did the dishes. No one liked being on dishes duty for a week! Girls in the fifth form served the staff table – this was to teach them from which side to serve and take away. The food was generally good but when it was macaroni cheese on the menu for supper I survived on bread and butter (I did not like cooked cheese!). We all had our own individual butter dishes and were allocated a quarter of a pound of butter per week which was kept in a cupboard, not a fridge. My favourite breakfasts were on Sundays and Wednesdays when we had cereal, soft bread rolls and a piece of fruit. Others liked the fried bread with tinned tomatoes which for some reason was called dead dog!

We had morning assembly, then lessons began with a break midmorning for cocoa and a biscuit in the winter and lemonade made from powder in the summer. More lessons followed until lunchtime. After lunch, we went to our form rooms, where a prefect would open our tuck cupboard. One piece of fruit and three to four sweets depending on the size, all brought from home, was our ration for the day. Once afternoon lessons were over we could have tea in the dining room if we wanted it; this meal consisted of bread and butter with jam or any other delicacy such as pate, cheese slices, peanut butter and the like, provided from home.

After tea was our allotted time for homework or prep as we called it and this was held in the library where we sat at folding desks placed in rows. I can still see the book *Murder in the Cathedral*, the story of Thomas Becket, staring at me from the shelves that I sat next to. Prep lasted one and a half hours after which we changed from our gym tunics into a kilt or green skirt, a shirt blouse made of a soft material resembling green denim with a school tie completing the outfit.

Another bell summoned us to evening prayers with supper following, after which we were free until bedtime. At the allotted time, we went to an anteroom outside the staff room, to say goodnight to the duty mistress who ticked off our names on the register. The school matron came around the dormitories to make sure that lights were off at the appropriate time and woe betide any noise afterwards.

A bath rota showed us the time of our twice weekly baths. Our bath slot was ten minutes! Therefore, we would clean the bath and start running the next person's bath before drying ourselves to make sure we all got as long a soak as possible. The rest of the week we were required to have strip washes. I cannot, now, believe that I was once agile enough to be able to get a foot into a washhand basin!

Three weeks after the start of term, we had an 'out weekend' when we were allowed to be out with our parents or other suitable adults, but not overnight. Before going out on the Saturday morning we did our usual one hour of prep, which was always a composition and then we were free to go out until suppertime. On Sunday we were allowed out all day until 5pm, returning in time for our evening service, taken by the headmistress, another member of staff or an outside speaker, maybe one of the local clergy. After supper those who wanted to could go to chorus singing in the library. We took it in turns to choose choruses out of the CSSM chorus book. I always went to this as it reminded me of home and going to Sunday school and I loved singing.

Half term was six weeks after the start of term and we went home for a long weekend, Friday morning until Monday evening. Another weekend of out days followed, three weeks later and after a further three weeks came the end of our 12-week term.

The weekends spent at school had a special routine of prep on Saturday morning followed by mending. When our clothes returned from the laundry, matron sorted and checked everything, and anything missing – a button, or a sock with a hole in it – she put into the mending basket. All those with mending assembled in the library, where we repaired our garments to the best of our ability and to the satisfaction of matron. Saturday afternoons were spent walking for two hours whatever the weather. A teacher led the walks until we were about fourteen or fifteen when we could go unsupervised, two or more girls together. After supper we had entertainment; each form took it in turns to provide this and when this was over, we had Scottish country dancing. Saturday evening was the one time we changed into a non-uniform dress and as we got older, high heels were acceptable!

Sunday meant we could have an extra hour in bed. On winter Sundays we dressed in our green serge dresses, which had a detachable cream collar, and in the summer green and white striped dresses. After breakfast we, assembled in the library for inspection before going to church: were shoes clean, were stocking seams straight and was our hair tidy? We then set off in twos in crocodile formation to walk to Minto Church. I did find the Church of Scotland rather different to Chapel at home but became quite used to it. By the time we had walked back to school, we were ready for Sunday dinner, which was always roast meat with roast potatoes and vegetables. After lunch, we wrote our weekly letter home, under the supervision of a mistress until we were older. Our letters given to the duty mistress were in an unsealed envelope with our initials on the back, presumably so that the staff could read them. Next was our Sunday afternoon walk lasting one hour, before returning for tea and cake; this was followed by our evening service, supper, then chorus singing.

One notable occasion in the school year was the harvest thanksgiving held shortly after returning to school in September; the gymnasium was the venue for this special service, being ideal as it was very easy to to decorate the wall bars at the back of the stage. Coloured leaves and berries provided a very attractive reminder of God being the Creator and Giver of all the good things that are celebrated at harvest time. Normally our Sunday evening services were held in the library but the gymnasium was used for other special events such as our carol service, concerts and prize giving

With my birthday being at the beginning of December, I always celebrated it at school. The ritual first thing in the morning as we stood in our house lines after assembly was to be 'dumped', that is, being thrown up in the air and caught by those who had thrown you, once for every year of your life. I don't think anybody was dropped! At tea time there was generally birthday cake that had been sent from home. Later in December, just before the end of term we would have our Christmas party, which in true party fashion we all got dressed up for in our party dresses. We all wore white dresses at our end of term carol service to which our parents were invited and likewise at our end of year concert.

The main event of the spring term was the gym competition when the houses competed. This I loathed. I enjoyed hockey and tennis and could have wished to be better at them but I certainly never aspired to being a gymnast. Any competition requires a lot of practice and there were only two suitable sites. The gymnasium, a purpose built wooden structure, was situated near to what had been the stables, (they housed the science laboratory, art room and domestic science kitchen). The other location was the library and as there were four houses, only two could practice at once, hence every other morning we got up in time for gym comp practices starting at 7am, not so good if it was your turn to head to the gymnasium when there stood a good chance of it being wintry weather.

The summer term ended with sports day and a final concert and prize giving which our parents came to and then it was Home Sweet Home!

I don't remember any pillow fights but I do remember a planned midnight feast. I say 'planned' because it never happened. We were discovered, or rather all the food that we had been hiding was, and we ended up being made to sit in sick bay under Matron's watchful eye and eat as much as we possibly could, until we all felt quite ill.

Ariel view of boarding school showing the rear of the building

Happy to be home for the holidays

8

The Reality of Death

WE ALL APPRECIATE that parents and teachers need to discipline children. It was no different at boarding school. There were four categories of offence. A late mark if one was late for classes. A confiscation mark, if the duty mistress when doing her rounds at night found any of your belongings out of place. For example, a hockey boot on the boot room floor instead of in your locker or any offending article, which was stopping your desk lid from closing. The next morning the reading of the confiscation list took place after breakfast; you then retrieved the offending article along with your confiscation mark. An order mark was given if you were rude to a teacher. Later you had the pleasure of informing your house captain who was not too pleased! If you had a certain number of these disciplinary marks in a week, you had to do detention on a Saturday night.Finally the fourth, the most serious of all was a conduct mark, given for gross misconduct which not only meant detention but if you received more than one of those in a term you were likely to be expelled.

Boarding school, did I enjoy it? My automatic response would be, no, I hated it. There were some enjoyable times but after the first few days, I became terribly homesick and would write home and say that if my parents didn't come and get me I would run away. In fact, thirty years later when I cleared out Mummy's desk, I found a letter from my headmistress telling my parents that unless I started to settle down during the second half of my first term, they would have to remove me from school at the end of term. If only I had known! I now realise that even the homesickness was part of God's plan for my life and I can look back and see the truth in Jeremiah chapter 29 verse 11: 'For I know the plans I have for you declares the Lord, plans to prosper you and not to harm you, plans to give you a hope and a future.'

As I have already said, I was always near the top of the class in primary school. However when I went to Craigmount I was put into a class that had already done one year of French and basic maths. Latin was a completely new subject to all of us. I struggled and combined with the homesickness it was a recipe for disaster. At the end of my first year, the school wanted to put me down a class. This I declined as I had made friends in my class and did not want any more changes in my life. I continued in that class for the rest of my time there making no attempt to work and getting terrible marks. The only thing I got high marks for was my posture and music exams with not so high marks but I never passed an aural test!

Mummy, Auntie Lah and I suppose Daddy were just as miserable at my being away. This state of affairs continued until January 1958 when I was fourteen. When I had been home for the Christmas holidays, it was apparent that Auntie Lah was not well. She was having trouble seeing the music when playing the organ and had temporarily stepped down from her position as organist. Mummy wanted her to come and stay with us for Christmas but she refused saying she would come after I had returned to school, as she wanted to sleep in my bedroom and that is what happened.

When I got up on Saturday 18th January 1958 little did I know that the events that would take place during the next week were to be life defining moments. I was in lower fifth form and we were now going on our weekend walks unsupervised. We would often walk to Denholm village to buy sweets with money drawn from our school bank accounts for which we all had our own cheque book. If we were walking to Denholm, we had to present ourselves to the duty mistress for inspection by a certain time. That Saturday in January 1958, a friend and I decided to do just that but unfortunately, we arrived for inspection after the allotted time. The duty mistress was no longer there. We decided to go anyway.

As well as shopping, I posted a picture postcard of red roses to Auntie Lah. While out we met some of the more senior girls, and this led to news of our outing reaching the staffroom. At assembly on Monday 20[th,] the whole school sat on the floor while the two of us stood. The headmistress announced that we were receiving conduct marks for going to Denholm without inspection first. This was gross disobedience. Our punishment was to be as follows: we would be going on the junior supervised walks every weekend, which was very humiliating; and we would also be doing detention on Saturday evenings for the rest of the term. What was detention? Well, there would be no Saturday evening entertainment, or country dancing for us for the rest of the term. Our Saturday evenings were to be spent sitting in a form room along with the duty mistress doing maths or some such awful subject. It was truly ghastly.

It was not a very good week but was set to get very much worse. On Friday 24th January I was summoned to the headmistress's room. Needless to say I wondered what else I had done wrong but this time she gave me the devastating news that my beloved Nanny (Auntie Lah) had died on the Wednesday. I was to go and find matron who would help me pack my suitcase as Daddy was coming to collect me.

Once home I heard that Auntie Lah had had a massive stroke, dying hours later in the General Hospital in Newcastle.

Later that day when Daddy and I took our dog Mickie for a walk, I confessed about my receiving a conduct mark. Daddy told me that they knew and not to worry.

He also told me how pleased Auntie Lah had been to receive the postcard with red roses on it. Later Mummy gave me a postcard that Auntie Lah had written in reply to mine the day before she died, which had not been posted.

Mummy was devastated as she and Auntie Lah had been extremely close. Grandfather and Auntie Flossie moved temporarily into 'West Rays' and I will never forget the sight of my grandfather weeping as he sat by the fire in our house. A cousin of Mummy's and his wife (Uncle Bill and Auntie Betty) arrived from Newcastle to stay with us and Auntie Betty was a great comfort to me.

The funeral was the first that I had attended and the whole situation was very unreal. I remember us driving through the village in the funeral car and Daddy walking in front of the hearse. Looking out of the car window and thinking how thoughtful the shopkeepers had been in closing their shops, completely forgetting that it was a Sunday afternoon and shops in those days closed on Sundays.

I knew that Auntie Lah had gone to be with Jesus as she had committed her life to Him when she was young, and that she was safe but oh, how I wanted her back with us. What would I do without her?

Auntie Lah

I went back to school the next weekend and continued to face the punishment for my disobedience.

Three weeks later it was half term and I went home to find Mummy had developed phlebitis and was generally not at all well. Auntie Lah gone, Mummy not well: I did not want to return to school. However, return I must, but on returning to school on the Monday evening I flatly refused to get out of the car! No cajoling by Daddy or members of staff could move me, and poor Daddy had to take me home. I returned later in the week.

During the second half of the term I developed a cough, which Matron treated with cough mixture. I was still coughing when I returned home for the Easter holidays so Mummy changed my medicine to her favourite potion.

My parents had decided to let 'West Rays' and along with my grandfather were busy clearing it, which to me was quite heartrending. I was trying to organise my things for school and was acutely aware of no Auntie Lah. She was the practical one and was now no longer there to support me.

My cough persisted and shortly before the end of the holidays I coughed up a large amount of blood. The doctor came and sent me to Alnwick Infirmary for a chest x-ray, which revealed that I had pneumonia; by this time I was extremely unwell, but we had a good doctor who treated me with the appropriate antibiotic. However, I was not able to return to school until after half term. This of course had an even more devastating effect on my schoolwork, which was pretty awful anyway.

My parents discussed my predicament with the headmistress and I was asked if I would like to leave school at Christmas, shortly after my fifteenth birthday. I jumped at the chance. December could not come soon enough: the end of a horrendous three and a half years.

Although I was unhappy I realise not everyone is able to have the experience of living in a stately home surrounded by beautiful grounds, which included a large lake and a stream flowing through. I will never forget the hundreds of baby frogs that emerged from the lake in summer – some girls put them in the beds of other girls! Then there was the beauty of the snow-covered trees in winter and all the wonderful walks. Independence was something else I learnt very quickly, there being no parent to pick up behind you or help find the lost shoe. However, in spite of these positive things I was certainly not sorry to leave.

Did I ever think about my adoption during my time at Craigmount? Yes I did. I can remember hearing the song 'Maybe it's because I'm a Londoner' and thinking that this probably applied to me as I had come from London. What's more, a friend recently reminded me of my fantasising that I was a Romanian princess. Why, would I think that? Well there was a girl a year or two above me at school called Despina. When Mummy had seen her name on a school programme, she told me that Despina was the name of the person that Auntie Martin knew who had connections with the adoption agency and that she was a princess. My fertile imagination thought that she might be a relation of mine. Was I a princess? Maybe not, perhaps I just had a cockney background. I have since learned that the tendency to fantasise is very common in people who know about their adoption but have no knowledge of their birth family and background.

9

What Next?

DECEMBER **1958** was bitter sweet; on the one hand I was leaving boarding school – how wonderful to be going home never again to return to school. On the other hand, I was going home to the first Christmas without Auntie Lah.

I don't remember too much about that Christmas apart from my Grandfather and Auntie Flossie coming to stay and that my Christmas present was a record player along with some records, one sounding very march like. Auntie Flossie amused us all when at breakfast she said, 'Oh! I thought it was a Boys Brigade band marching down the road!'

January 1959 dawned and with it the realisation that I was not going back to school. What was I going to do to fill the days? Mummy was not at all well so helping at home was a priority and I was to continue with my piano lessons.

As most of my clothes were school uniform, a shopping expedition was called for and provided a pleasant interlude.

I must say I enjoyed doing housework, cooking, etc. My Father was still running his funeral directing business, which he had set up after returning to Seahouses. This meant the household could be very busy as he was on call 24/7 often needing meals at unusual times, which was no problem for Mummy as our meals were never on time and were sometimes referred to as moveable feasts!

Joan, my best friend since before primary school, had left the village due to the relocation of her father's work and of course, I really missed her. Fortunately, one of my other close friends named Pamela still lived in Bamburgh and we soon resumed our friendship. Pamela went to the grammar school in Alnwick so we saw each other at weekends and school holidays.

Pamela and I did a lot of cycling and on one memorable occasion, we cycled to a spot near Howick about ten miles south of Seahouses to visit two boys who were camping there. One boy was the Presbyterian minister's son (Pamela attended the Presbyterian Church) and a friend of his. The boys were unaware of our impending visit and were not there. By the time the boys returned, we realised we were not going to make it home before lighting up time. Unfortunately, we did not have lights on our bikes! How thankful we were that the boys' bikes were equipped with lights. The problem was solved – we would borrow their bikes and they would ride ours back to Seahouses the next day and retrieve theirs. Pamela and I set off for home but having had very little to eat or drink we were extremely hungry and thirsty. By the time we reached the village of Embleton, we decided to try to buy a drink, but from where? We ventured into The Dunstanburgh Castle Hotel bar with only a small amount of money and me feeling very guilty as both of my parents were teetotal. However, we managed to buy lemonade and were able to make a telephone call home to say that we were safe. I should say at this stage that nobody had known of our plans for that afternoon! Refreshed, we continued, the only other excitement being when I ran into a wall and came off the bike. Fortunately no damage was done to either me, or the bike and eventually we arrived back home relieved, tired and rather chastened by our telling off from parents.

Another favourite pastime was playing tennis on the courts at Bamburgh. We thoroughly enjoyed ourselves except when the local boys came to watch and cheer us on. Pamela was cheered on by 'Come on Miss... and her surname'; I got

'Come on Miss Happy Joe' which was really embarrassing to say the least since my Father was known in the area as 'Happy Joe.' I suspect it started in Eyemouth, consequently following him back to Northumberland. The name suited his personality and recently two people have referred to him by that name.

Spring 1960 saw me embark on what I suppose for me was quite an adventure. Aged sixteen, I travelled on my own from Newcastle to London en route for Torquay where I was to spend Easter visiting relatives. Mummy had accompanied me as far as Newcastle. The journey to Devon took a very long time and a stopover in London was required. Therefore, after sixteen years I was back in London where I had presumably been born. How convenient it was that Auntie Mabel lived in London and this was to be the first of several visits to her home. Auntie Mabel knew London very well and was a very informative guide and I loved it! She took me to all the main London sites. I especially remember listening to the bells of St. Clements Dane ringing out the tune of 'Oranges and Lemons'; also a concert in The Royal Festival Hall. Magnolia trees were completely new to me as was a cream tea, which we enjoyed at the roof gardens in Derry and Toms department store on Kensington High Street.

My holiday in Torquay was much enjoyed as the relatives there were very close to both sides of my family and one of them was around my age so we had lots of fun together.

Life continued as before but I was now taking one of the primary age Sunday school classes, which I found rather daunting, as they were boys; in fact, I never seemed to have a girls' class.

During the summer of 1960, Pamela invited me to go with her to a Young Presbyterian house party in Yorkshire where we really enjoyed ourselves and attended another one the following Easter.

In December 1960 I reached the very important age of seventeen and applied for my provisional driving license, the gateway to more freedom and independence! My first time behind the wheel was at a disused aerodrome on a local farm with Daddy sitting beside me. After a few circuits of the aerodrome he told me to stop. After stopping, Daddy proceeded to get out of the car and said, 'On you go' – so on I went with only some sheep to get in the way, which I happily managed to avoid.

As I was to have proper driving lessons after the New Year in Berwick-upon-Tweed, I asked my parents if I could enrol for a secretarial course also in Berwick. They said yes, so the course was booked and I travelled on the bus twice a week to Berwick for both sets of lessons. I have to admit that my driving was a much bigger success than my shorthand. Secretarial work was not for me. (How amusing as I sit typing this page.) Mummy certainly appreciated my driving ability, as she no longer had to depend on Daddy to drive her around in connection with her Bible Society and Scripture Union work. This I enjoyed but at times I did feel that it would be good to have some real employment or a training of some kind. That might involve leaving home again and I was not ready for that.

During the summer of 1961 Pamela went with me to a Bible Society house party for young people and we ventured further afield than Yorkshire, going far south to Limpsfield in Surrey, from where I had another visit to London. We spent two weeks in Limpsfield and had a wonderful time, learning about the work of the Bible Society and having daily bible study groups. There was lots of fun and games as well and the making of new friends, some of whom I am still in touch with. One of these new friends was Maggie who came from Essex; although many miles apart we remained very good friends, visiting each other in our respective homes.

In 1962, still feeling the need to be either employed or to train for something, I was very interested to see an advert in the *Newcastle Journal*. This was for a temporary post in Newcastle-upon-Tyne to be nanny to a small boy eighteen months old. I applied, had an interview and got the post. This gave me a great sense of achievement after having so much failure in my life. Nannying definitely pushed me into uncharted waters, as I had no experience of very small children; however, he was a very sweet little boy and well behaved. His mother really needed my help as she had just had major surgery while being pregnant with her second child. Later I returned after the arrival of the new baby. I enjoyed the experience including nappy washing, but decided that being a Nanny was not for me.

Pamela was making plans to go to Edinburgh where she was to train as a nurse. Once more, I became unsettled, with my desire for some sort of training increasing, but what? So life continued as before.

At one point, I happened to mention to Mummy that a friend of mine had a friend called Noel. Mummy's response was interesting; she said, 'You were called Noelle when we adopted you. We liked the name but were advised to change it to something else.' Consequently, my parents named me after both of my grandmothers. Another piece of the jigsaw had just been slotted into place! Knowing my birth name seemed to deepen the sense of being two people, a feeling shared I imagine by many others in a similar situation.

In March 1963 my Wooler grandfather died, aged 89. This was another break in the family and those traditions associated with that part of my life. Grandfather always called me Jock, as he did all other children. Perhaps I should have been a boy! At some point during these years I can remember my grandfather bringing friends to visit and after introducing me, he turned to them and said, 'Of course she's not theirs.' I expect he thought

I wouldn't be listening! Well, I was, and that certainly made me wonder to whom I belonged.

That summer saw me head off firstly to Essex to stay with Maggie and then on to Burnham-on-Sea to another Bible Society house party. This time we went for four weeks, working the first two. I chose to work in the dining room/kitchen, which I enjoyed and Maggie worked with the children. The second two weeks we were on holiday at the youth house party, which was fun and it was great meeting up again with those I had met at Limpsfield.

In September of that year I received an invitation to a twenty-first birthday party of someone within the farming community. As they were all busy harvesting, they asked if I could meet someone from the train at Berwick-upon-Tweed station; his name was Addie Harkess. Apparently, Addie was going to be M.C. so would it be possible for him to borrow one of my father's top hats! I was quite happy to oblige. The party was a great success and whilst conversing with Addie I mentioned that a few weeks later I was having my wisdom teeth extracted in an Edinburgh Nursing Home. It just so happened that the Nursing Home was very near to Addie's office and I had a very pleasant surprise visit from him. I must have looked awful with my face being very swollen and bruised! Addie was very attentive, bringing me books, flowers and chocolates for when I could eat normally.

I had recently been very interested in someone else who was not a Christian and Daddy had seen fit to intervene, causing me much heartache. Daddy had at least two possible husbands lined up for me but I had no romantic feelings for them and I am sure it was mutual! The need to spread my wings became much more apparent and I had several ideas about what I might train for, but they all needed school leaving qualifications and I had none so what could I possibly do?

In the spring of 1964 there was an article in our local paper about a new State Enrolled Nursing course that had recently started. This was a two-year course and no formal qualifications were required. This was an interesting development. I had often played hospitals with my dolls when a child, especially after our visits to my grandfather who was in Newcastle General Hospital for quite a while when I was small. Moreover, I enjoyed looking after people. Could this be the answer to future employment? I would love to say that I prayed about the situation but I can't remember doing so. All I remember is the need to have some sort of training and a balanced life like other people of my age. Showing the article to my parents, I found them to be very supportive and they encouraged me to find out more. I wrote to the main hospitals in Newcastle and Edinburgh enquiring as to whether they were offering this course. The replies were that Newcastle had not so far started the S.E.N. course but the reply from the Royal Infirmary Edinburgh said that they had already begun to offer the course and were enclosing an application form, which I duly completed and posted with the required references.

A few weeks later I sat outside the office of the Lady Superintendent of Nurses waiting for an interview, my hands clammy just as they might be prior to a music exam. I wondered what she would think of me. The only interview I had ever had was for the post of nanny so I had no idea what to expect. Thankfully, the interview proved successful and I was offered a place in the September Preliminary Training School. It was helpful that Pamela was already training at R.I.E. and a boarding school friend was training in the city as well. Auntie Jean (my father's youngest sister) and her husband, Uncle George, lived in the city too. It was somewhere that I was very familiar with as we visited frequently.

Once more, there was great excitement at the prospect of beginning a new chapter of my life but this was a different kind of excitement to that of the eleven-year-old girl going off to boarding school. I was embarking on this venture because I wanted to, and I was ready to leave home.

Another trip to Edinburgh was required but not to purchase school uniform. This was to purchase the requirements needed to start nursing: two pairs of black lacing shoes, black stockings, a nurse's watch, scissors, with my name engraved on them and two large white laundry bags with a red panel on the front on which my name was embroidered in white.

Having everything in place for my new start in September I once again went off south, firstly to Devon to visit our relatives there and then on to Penzance where Maggie joined me for another four weeks with the Bible Society.

This brought to a close the second decade of my life in which there had been some highs and many lows. Integrating back into the village community after being at boarding school was difficult. My parents did not allow me to do things that might have made me more acceptable and my decision to follow Jesus was certainly put to the test, with my faith having many ups and downs.

10

Career, Courtship and Matrimony

EARLY SEPTEMBER 1964 saw me arriving at the preliminary training school of the Royal Infirmary Edinburgh. The building was in a pleasant road next to the infirmary and was comprised of several terraced houses. This was to be my home for the next few weeks. We all had our own bedrooms and there was a communal lounge and classrooms. Five of us were about to start the S.E.N. course, the rest were to do the Registered General Nursing course (R.G.N.) but at this stage we did everything together.

On the first day, we excitedly dressed in our uniforms, cotton dresses in green for S.E.N. and blue for R.G.N., starched white aprons and caps, black stockings and shoes with a scarlet cape to be worn outside going between wards. P.T.S. (preliminary training school,) was very enjoyable; we were lectured by sister tutors and practised making beds, bandaging, giving cardiac resuscitation to a dummy, etc. We also enjoyed going out to see how milk was pasteurised at a local dairy and to a water treatment works all in an attempt to teach us about public health.

After six weeks in P.T.S. we did a written test following which we commenced our practical training on our first ward. At this point, the Lady Superintendent of Nurses asked to see me and I wondered what I could possibly have done wrong! I need not have worried as she was offering me the chance to transfer to the R.G.N. course.

I thought about this offer but decided to turn it down, as I was unsure as to how I would manage the academic side of the course and I had no wish to relive my boarding school experience.

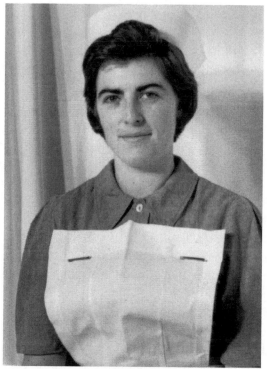

Esther in nurse's uniform

I soon became friends with a girl from Middlesborough who over the years has remained a very good friend although now many miles away in Hampshire. Angela is a Roman Catholic so we went our separate ways regarding church. However, two other girls were Methodists and the three of us started attending Methodist Central Hall, which was nearby, and sometimes another Methodist Church in the vicinity. I soon realised that Methodism in Edinburgh was rather different to what I had been used to in Northumberland, and after a few months I made my way to Charlotte Baptist Chapel, which I was familiar with having heard the pastor speak at a convention in Longhorsley, Northumberland, which I attended most years with my family.

About this time we were all moved from our pleasant P.T.S. accommodation into the old nurses' home which was quite different; my room looked onto the hospital laundry, whereas Angela's room looked onto a side street.

My first ward was a female medical and I can still recall some of those patients. After a few weeks, Pamela came to work on the same ward and a new working relationship was required, which was quite odd!

The beginning of December saw me celebrating my twenty-first birthday. I was on an early shift and in the evening all the girls took over the lounge in the nurses' home for a party. Mummy had sent me a birthday cake and we enjoyed this plus other party food. My parents had decided I would have a party for relatives and friends when I was on holiday the next February.

Shortly before Christmas I had a telephone call from Addie Harkess. I was rather surprised as I had had no communication with him since being in the nursing home. Addie had heard that I was in Edinburgh and he was calling to invite me to have dinner with him on Christmas Eve. I knew I was on an early shift that day so I was able to accept his invitation, which was a very pleasant surprise. Christmas Eve arrived and Addie took me to a lovely restaurant called The Handsel in Edinburgh's west end. We sat at a table for two beside a log fire and enjoyed traditional Christmas fare. As I was on an early shift on Christmas Day, I needed to be back at a reasonable hour, which I was. On returning I discovered that several of the girls were about to go to St. Giles Cathedral for the midnight carol service so off I went as well! Arriving back at the nurse's home we decided to open our Christmas presents. This meant that I got very little sleep before rising at an extremely early hour, to join with other nurses who were going carol singing around the wards. This was something of a tradition and everyone entered into the Christmas spirit. We then reported for duty at seven thirty!

In Scotland, the printing of newspapers still took place on Christmas Day and on that Christmas Day, I along with Pamela and several other girls, featured in a photograph on the front page of *The Scotsman* newspaper. The photographer took the photograph a few days earlier when we formed a group, singing carols around the large Christmas tree located at the foot of the wide sweeping staircase in the main surgical corridor.

We ate Christmas dinner on the ward, or rather in a temporary dining room, the patients' sitting room! I eventually went off duty around 5pm, telephoned my parents and then got ready to go out for my third Christmas dinner in twenty-four hours! I spent a very enjoyable evening at The Old Waverly Hotel on Princes Street in the company of Mummy's cousin and her husband from Wooler who usually spent Christmas there. As you can imagine I was very relieved to be on a late shift on Boxing Day.

It is abundantly clear that I had a very full and happy time over my first Christmas away from home. However, I really felt for my parents who were having Christmas on their own for the first time. I had been home shortly before Christmas leaving gifts for Mummy and Daddy and returned to visit them on my next days off.

In February 1965 I had my first holiday since beginning to train and I of course was to have my delayed 21st birthday party on the last Saturday of the month. This date coincidentally was

27th February, the birth date of my maternal grandmother and namesake, Esther.

Knowing that Addie had good M.C. skills I was encouraged by a friend to ask if he would help with my party, which he kindly agreed to and naturally, we met to plan the evening. On this occasion, Addie took me out to dinner at a very nice hotel in Kinross.

My party venue was a small hotel in Seahouses, where numerous relatives and friends from all over the country came to celebrate my coming of age. On my return to Edinburgh, I went to work at Corstorphine Hospital right next to the zoo! Addie and I met sometime in March to reminisce and look at photographs of the party and before we parted, he asked me to go to a concert in the Usher Hall. We duly went to the concert after having a meal at a nearby restaurant and from then on we continued to see each other regularly.

Training to be a nurse, I encountered many different experiences, some good, others not so good. Ward sisters could be extremely difficult, some colleagues hard to get along with, some patients were seriously ill, some died. All this was new to me. These situations certainly encouraged me to pray and I was to become very aware of the truth in one of Mummy's favourite quotations: 'More things are wrought by prayer than this world dreams of'—from Tennyson's 'Mort d'Arthur'.

During this time, I really benefited from the Bible teaching at Charlotte Chapel and at Elcho Place Hall in Port Seton where I would go with Addie if I was off duty on a Sunday evening; if I had a whole weekend off I would normally go home.

At the end of my first year of training I was once again asked if I would like to transfer to the R.G.N. course but again I declined; I was so enjoying the excellent marks that I managed to attain that I wanted in no way to spoil that sense of achievement.

Angela and I had decided to go on holiday together, having great fun choosing a destination with a suitable price tag! We set off for Austria, firstly on the overnight bus from Edinburgh to London, which I joined in Alnwick and Angela in Darlington. We did not have much sleep so were very tired on our arrival in London but we did manage to see the main sites. We also visited Auntie Mabel in St. Mary's Hospital, Paddington, where she was seriously ill and sadly, it was to be the last time that I saw her. Later that evening we were to stay with a family friend of Angela's. We arrived at the friend's house to find no one at home. We hung around and walked up and down the road but they did not return! What should we do?

We telephoned the YWCA to no avail. We went back to King's Cross station. Fortunately, I had much to Daddy's annoyance, taken my cheque book with me (he thought I would lose it) and this enabled me to book us into The Great Northern Hotel for bed and breakfast! How wonderful those beds felt, but not for very long as we had to be up extremely early the next morning in order to arrive at Victoria coach station to join our tour party. We had breakfast courtesy of room service, Angela freaking out when the waiter arrived and she was still in bed with rollers in her hair!

Our visit to Austria included taking the cable car up the nearby mountain, having a trip to the Dolomites across the Italian border and tasting the most delicious peaches. On the return journey, we experienced a massive thunderstorm with torrential rain in a leaking coach! We arrived back in Edinburgh in time to begin our second year of training, having thoroughly enjoyed our holiday.

Sometime later in September, Addie, prior to going on holiday was spending a weekend at Seahouses with my family and me. We were sitting in his blue mini parked on the drive at Romany, when he asked me to marry him (very romantic!) and

I had no hesitation in saying yes. He did ask my parents for their approval and they gave us their blessing. We made the decision to wait until my 22nd birthday that December to announce our engagement.

At some point prior to Addie's proposal I had told him the story of my adoption as I realised that I had in fact two backgrounds and one was completely unknown. He lovingly said that it made no difference.

Life was exciting. We went to choose an engagement ring and started making plans as to when the wedding would take place and where we might live. My birthday fell on a Sunday that year and I was on an early shift finishing at lunchtime. Addie came and collected me from the nurse's home and officially put our engagement ring onto my finger. I was now the very proud owner of a simple diamond solitaire that sparkled beautifully.

Now officially engaged we went to see Addie's mother who was visiting her sister in a village to the south of Edinburgh, after which we continued on to Seahouses to see my parents. It was a wonderful day in my life.

The following year of 1966 seemed to fly past and I left R.I.E. in December, having completed my training. I returned home to Seahouses and at the beginning of January, 1967, I started a temporary post doing permanent night duty at Alnwick Infirmary. It was something of a culture shock going from a large teaching hospital to such a small one where they were yet to install bedpan washers! There were three wards and two single rooms that night sister and I looked after. If we needed to have a body moved to the mortuary, we had to phone for the police, as there was no porter on duty during the night! We also had to cook our own meals in the ward kitchen so nights were busy and varied.

Our wedding was planned for the end of April so having several days off at one time was very advantageous. I must say

Mummy was wonderful at making telephone calls while I was in bed sleeping! Mummy, having decided to make the wedding cake, made five in all. The first one was a trial, then the cakes for the three tiers plus an extra one for cutting. The recipe was my grandmother Esther's which had been made for her own wedding and Mummy's. The cakes when baked were then taken to our local baker who iced them very simply after which white ribbons were tied around each cake.

Fenwick's in Newcastle was where I went with Mummy to choose my wedding dress, and a wonderfully, exciting expedition it proved to be. We knew one of the buyers and she came to give her opinion as well. The dress that I chose was long and straight and with a full-length train falling from the shoulders; it was made of white crepe and trimmed with guipure lace. Having looked at bridesmaids' dresses in a similar style and material it was then necessary for Pamela and Maggie who were going to be my bridesmaids, to go shopping with me for their dresses. We chose a lovely shade of sky blue, which suited them both, but were to have a panic about getting their shoes dyed to match. Eventually they became a reality. Now I needed to choose the material for Sheila's dress (Addie's nine-year-old niece). For this I went with Addie's sister Marion to Jenners, the famous Edinburgh department store, where she was a dressmaker. Marion had agreed to make the dress in the same style as the adult bridesmaids. We decided on a crepe material in a shade of pale primrose, also buying lace that would be dyed to match.

Paxton and Purves in Berwick-on-Tweed was the destination for Mummy to choose her wedding outfit. I even persuaded her back into high-heeled shoes! Her chosen outfit was a matching dress and coat made of wool georgette, the colour of pale sea-haze. Her beautiful brown straw hat was trimmed with pale pink roses and her new brown shoes with matching bag and gloves completed her outfit.

For my bouquet I chose lily of the valley, white freesias, stephanotis and pale pink orchids and Mummy's corsage was made of similar orchids. The florist in Alnwick where Daddy had always ordered funeral flowers from had agreed to make a matching hair band for me. I have always loved polyanthus for their wonderful colour range and velvety petals and I especially wanted my bridesmaids to carry posies of these delightful flowers and to have matching hair bands too. The florist was doubtful about the hair bands but she very kindly experimented and announced that they should last for the required amount of time. Phew!

Addie and I, having decided to live in Edinburgh, went house hunting, and about three weeks prior to the wedding, we became owners of a small bungalow on the south side of the city. It was in good condition though somewhat dated in décor but we looked forward to choosing our own colour schemes and furniture and turning it into a home.

The day prior to the wedding was a hive of activity with various people coming to stay, not with us, but in bed and breakfast accommodation. From teatime on, we ran a buffet, which Mummy and I had prepared for all visitors who required food. Addie and I were able to slip away on the pretext of meeting bridesmaids from the train, which we eventually did. However prior to that, having left in separate cars, our destination was Bamburgh, where I had previously arranged to hide Addie's car in the village garage. Mission accomplished, we then set off for Chathill station, returning home with the said bridesmaids and looking very innocent as to where else we had been! Later on in the evening, we had a rehearsal and I was able to see the flowers, which Auntie Cissie and two other relatives were busy arranging in Chapel. I had chosen white narcissi (pheasant's eye, a favourite of mine) along with blue irises and yellow tulips interspersed with suitable greenery.

I awoke on the 29th April to the most glorious day, brilliant sunshine with not a cloud in the sky and so it remained for the rest of the day with just a slight breeze off the sea. We were up reasonably early as we had early hairdressing appointments. The wedding service was at 12.30pm. Everything was going to plan, the flowers arrived on time and after coffee and a snack, it was time to dress for the wedding. Yes, everything was going well – until I put on my dress. 'Oh no!' I realised that the buttons on my suspenders could be seen through the material! My heart sank – why had I not noticed before? I was horrified, and near to tears when Pamela said, 'Take your girdle off and turn it outside in, then the buttons will be next to your leg and won't be seen.' It worked! Pamela had well and truly fulfilled her role as bridesmaid. From then on things did go according to plan.

We were married at Seahouses Methodist Chapel. The minister, the Rev. Kenneth Alton, conducted the marriage ceremony and Uncle John, Auntie Mabel's brother, gave the address just as his father had done at the marriage of my parents. We finished by singing a hymn praising God for everything in the past and trusting Him for everything in the future. After the signing of the register during which a friend sang, we emerged to the sound of Mendelssohn's wedding march to walk down the aisle as Mr and Mrs Adam Harkess.

The usual crowd of local wedding watchers were waiting for us to emerge from Chapel. After the taking of photos Addie threw the customary scramble money onto the road for the local children. Then it was off on a short drive to the reception, which was in a restaurant overlooking the sea.

Following more photographs, a lovely meal, Mummy's delicious wedding cake and the obligatory speeches, we went back to Romany to change. I had no problem changing; Pamela and Maggie were on hand to help, but Addie took far longer! At his home in Port Seton Addie had very sensibly taken the precaution of keeping his going away suit locked up inside his wardrobe. I had hung it in the spare bedroom at Romany ready for him to change into. However, his elder sister Catherine had other ideas. It was payback time! Catherine had gone to a tremendous amount of trouble and had taken the back off Addie's wardrobe in order to locate his suit and had stitched it up, leaving no way for him to get into it. A pair of scissors was called for, or perhaps that should be shouted for! We were eventually driven away only to be pursued by more persons wanting to get their own back on Addie. Our driver did her best but we had to change cars. This time we were driven by a friend of Addie's who had no axe to grind with him; however, the pursuants didn't give up easily and we took off on a mammoth car chase along the Northumberland country lanes, arriving back in Bamburgh when all those pursuing us had eventually given up. At last, we were able to retrieve the car and start out for our honeymoon destination in Perthshire.

We of course have wonderful memories of our honeymoon but there are other memories too. The weather included snow, hailstones and thunder and lightning; but, just imagine going down to dinner and discovering three ladies that we knew seated at the table next to ours!

Addie and Esther's wedding

My bridesmaids

11

Parenting

AFTER OUR WEDDING we soon settled down in our new home, really enjoying redecorating and furnishing it and using the lovely wedding presents that so many people had given us. Some were from local people who had known us as we grew up in our respective villages, very much a village tradition. I am still using a potato peeler that an elderly lady in Seahouses gave to me as a wedding present! However, I soon discovered that we were not the first to open packets of sheets, towels, etc. Catherine had beaten us to it; she must have spent a small fortune on confetti!

I soon returned to work, doing part time night duty at the Royal Infirmary Edinburgh. We started worshipping at a small fellowship in the Morningside area of Edinburgh known as the Old Schoolhouse as indeed that is what it had been. The clock on the outside of the building was stopped at the time that the last children left the building when it ceased to be a school, and it remained that way for many years. Fortunately, a member of the fellowship being an engineer was able to restore the working parts and so the clock once more told the time as it does to this present day. Addie soon became involved in the Sunday school and a midweek boys' club.

During the summer of 1968 we were delighted to tell our families and friends that we were expecting our first baby. This is another life-changing event in any family. For me I longed for this child who would actually be part of me and I certainly felt the deep sense of not belonging, although Addie would always say 'but you belong to me'; of course that was true and more importantly I rediscovered what it meant to be completely secure in my loving Heavenly Father's love for me. However, when attending the antenatal clinic the feeling of there being something missing was profound, especially the lack of family medical history when being asked if my parents were still alive and if not what their cause of death had been. For me this was an unanswerable question and prompted fresh thoughts as to who my birth parents were; were they in fact still alive and did they ever think about me? I didn't think that they would be together and presumed my mother to have been very young when I was born with the possibility of my father not surviving the war.

In the middle of April 1969 I gave birth to our baby son, Christopher Adam. Did he look like me? Well, nobody knew what I had looked like at birth or during the first few weeks of my life; nobody on my side of the family could say, 'I remember when you were born.' I could not comprehend how any mother could have given away their baby; my birth mother must have had a very good reason and it must have been terrible for her, unless she had really wanted rid of me. The void in my life had just increased.

Christopher was a very good contented baby who really did what all the baby books said and the three of us quickly settled down into a new family routine. Addie became chief bottle maker after my decision not to breast feed; I saw no reason to do so as I had never been breast fed, and seemed to have survived quite well without.

The following spring not long after Christopher's first birthday Daddy became unwell. Following admission to the infirmary in Edinburgh, tests revealed that he had an enlarged heart and a leaking valve. Mummy stayed with us, as they both did following my father's discharge from hospital. They stayed on until he had his first check up when a further complication, an aortic aneurysm, became apparent. Surgery was out of the question because of his age and other medical conditions. Mummy described the next two years as living on the edge of a precipice.

In September, 1971, we moved to our present home about a ten-minute walk from where we were then living. We now had an extra bedroom, which made life easier when my parents came to stay which was often.

We visited Seahouses frequently, seeing each other about every three weeks. On these visits to Seahouses my father and Christopher were always together, going for walks with the current Yorkshire terrier called Timmy. These walks would be up the old railway line opposite Romany and through North Sunderland, with my father buying Christopher an ice cream on the way back. This then resulted in a visit to Auntie Annie who still lived up the road but no longer had the shop. This was necessary so that Christopher could have all traces of ice cream removed before returning home to Romany, lest I should see the evidence! The other very necessary activity was for my father to read books to Christopher.

Mummy fed the local blackbirds with sultanas and soon found she had a small human that enjoyed them too! Her early morning bread and butter proved very popular as well.

The couple who rented West Rays at that time were more than pleased for Christopher to visit and he ran back and forth to West Rays just as I had done. People in the village said they would know which house to return Christopher to if he should get lost – there must have been some resemblance to me!

My father could no longer mow the lawns or cut the hedges so Addie took on these tasks as well as our now much larger garden plus at times helping in his mother's garden at Port Seton.

The first Christmas in our new home was lovely. We not only had Grandpa and Grandma (my parents) staying with us but Granny (Addie's mother) staying as well and Auntie Jean and Uncle George came to spend Christmas Day with us too.

In April 1972 my parents came for Christopher's third birthday when his nursery school friend came to tea along with Granny. Sadly, this was to be my father's last visit to Edinburgh, as he died very suddenly, but not unexpectedly, the following month; far better for him, but leaving a larger than life gap in our family. Just before he was admitted to hospital two years previously, the minister from chapel visited him and asked if he was afraid of dying, to which my father replied, 'Absolutely not, it will be the greatest adventure of all!' How wonderful to have that assurance. He also told us to sing the Hallelujah chorus from Handel's Messiah at his funeral! We did the next best thing and sang a hymn ending in 'Hallelujah, what a saviour!' and these are the words that are inscribed on the headstone on my parent's grave.

On Mummy's birthday in August of that year we were able to give her the news that another baby was on the way which gave her and of course us something wonderful to look forward to. Christmas that year was very strange, there being only four of us, as Granny was spending Christmas with Addie's youngest sister Marion who now had a baby girl. Auntie Jean and Uncle George who had unfortunately had a heart attack a few months earlier, decided to spend Christmas quietly at home.

In March 1973 Auntie Cissie died very suddenly and I was so sad that I could not attend her funeral, as our baby was due very shortly. She had been so much part of my life and would have loved to meet our new baby. She and Auntie Lah had worked together as volunteers for many years at the village baby clinic, held in the Sunday school room at Chapel. There they sold the baby food and orange juice to the Mums, and I loved it when I somtetimes went with them during the school holidays.

The new baby, who we named Sarah Elizabeth Jane, decided to keep us waiting, arriving six days late at the beginning of April. Now life changed dramatically. We three were now four and the new addition was not the contented baby that Christopher had been. Alas, Christopher had also developed a habit over the previous year of getting up several times during the night. More often than not Addie was the only one in bed asleep!

When Sarah was nine months old Mummy fell and broke her humerus, which meant a lengthy stay with us, as she could not live on her own. However, Timmy the Yorkshire terrier being present encouraged Sarah to start crawling; fortunately he was tiny and made many escapes to safety hiding under furniture.

The next notable event was the sudden death of Uncle George in February 1976 after which in a very short space of time, Granny had a stroke while staying with Addie's sister Catherine. Thankfully, she made a good recovery, being able to return to her own home.

It was becoming increasingly evident that Mummy needed to be near us and at the beginning of 1977 she bought a house in the next road to us. Quite soon after, Granny had another stroke, which was very severe and she was not expected to survive. Amazingly, she did and this was to herald our many years of hospital visiting.

Mummy, having decided to move near to us, weekly visits to Seahouses became the norm for me. I left home as soon as Addie returned from work on a Friday, returning early Sunday morning so that he could get to Sunday school. My mother hoarded so there was much to clear out especially with her moving to a much smaller house. One pleasant interlude was the wedding of Addie's niece Sheila but the next day Sarah went down with chickenpox. In fact, I think she had it at the wedding! Unknown to me, of course – I thought she had an insect bite! She had been abnormally quiet but the following morning there were more spots and a consultation with our next-door neighbour who was a retired doctor confirmed my suspicions. Christopher also caught the dreaded pox and both children had it quite badly.Grounded, just when I was dealing with tradesmen at Mummy's new house and having to look for carpets, etc. It wasn't much fun. I also found the move from Romany to be extremely emotional as did poor Mummy who said, 'I will only come back once' – and I knew that she meant that it would be at the end of her life. I too have never been back inside Romany. Although I have been back many times to the village, I prefer to remember my childhood home as it was. I am glad that Sarah has some memories of it as well as Christopher. Apparently Sarah's most vivid memory is the cooing of woodpigeons. I am also glad that she knew what it was to run back and forth between Romany and West Rays.

Later that summer we started an extension to our house, which we had been planning prior to Mummy's move, thinking that she could come and spend the winters with us. Now there was no need for it but having thought it through we decided to go ahead as we wanted a spare bedroom. The work began and we lived a rather hectic life for several months, but over the years it has proved to be a beneficial decision.

Mummy came to stay with us over Christmas and Addie's sister Margaret came to Christmas dinner, after which we all went to visit Granny who was at this stage in Astley Ainslie Hospital where she had gone for rehabilitation. Mummy enjoyed herself while we visited Granny, there being a piano in the corridor where she played Christmas carols.

This first decade of marriage was certainly one of many changes and we could certainly agree with our final wedding hymn, praising God for all that was past and comitting the future to Him.

12

Papers Discovered

JANUARY 1978 began with Granny moving to a geriatric ward at the Royal Infirmary, a ward I knew well having often done relief night duty there. Since having my children, I no longer nursed as my time was taken up with other things and I had recurring back problems.

Later that summer we said goodbye to Timmy, a much loved pet. I was so glad that Mummy had been able to have him with her at the beginning of what must have been quite a traumatic change in her life. Not long after, Auntie Phemie, an old friend of Mummy's, came over from Canada for a visit. This coincided with Sarah starting primary school. Mummy and Auntie Phemie both having been teachers were very interested in the modern teaching methods and took great delight in seeing the new words that appeared every day in a little tin box.

Thinking how nice it would be to have a dog in the family again, we decided to go and see a red setter puppy; he was beautiful, and of course, we just had to have him join the family. We really went from the sublime to the ridiculous concerning the difference in size between a Yorkshire terrier and a red setter. I remember the vet saying that he would grow into his paws! Indeed Jasper did grow into a magnificent dog and to see him run on the nearby field was comparable to watching a racehorse at speed.

Setters are notoriously scatty and often destructive. Jasper was sometimes scatty but not very destructive; even as a puppy, we only had one sandal and a hat chewed! Alas, that changed the last year of his life when he became senile and we could no longer leave him in the house alone. The scatty side manifested itself in numerous ways, especially concerning certain items of washing. I did Mummy's washing and Granny's washing came mostly to us, as we were the members of the family living in Edinburgh. I don't know if dogs can differentiate between colours but I am sure Jasper could, as he seemed to favour a certain nightdress belonging to Granny. It was pink and every time it was on the washing line, Jasper would take a mad turn, flying around the garden with the said nightdress in his mouth having pulled it from the washing line. He never took anything else from the washing line but he did do the same thing with a rose bush, which also happened to be pink – replanting was often required.

I think God must have known that I needed a dog in my life and provided me with Jasper because our daily dog walk became an oasis of calm in what was a very busy and often stressful life.

Over the next few years Mummy deteriorated cognitively and became increasingly manipulative in seeking my attention. During 1981 the doctor decided it would be a good idea for her to go to a day centre two days a week at a nearby hospital. This idea was often more bother than it was worth. Mummy would be very slow in getting ready so that no sooner had I left her there than it was time to return and collect her. This came to a climax when a nurse from our local psychiatric hospital decided that when a bed became available, it would be wise to admit Mummy to the unit. I knew she would never go willingly but the nurse told me that they would just come and take her. I agonised over this and decided that when the time came I would say no and find some other way. There would be no easy solution to our problems.

I prayed that if it was God's will, that Mummy should be in long term care, that He would make it easy for her to accept this. Our prayers are sometimes answered in the way we least expect or want. Sometimes the answer is no and sometimes it is wait. Whichever way it is, it is always for our good even though we do not see it at the time.

In this case I did not have long to wait. About two weeks later Mummy became unwell with an infection. Her home help, and another two ladies who I employed privately to help with her, were all off with similar infections. This led to the doctor saying that no one else was to go into the house but me. The next five days were amazing. Mummy was much more like her old self and of course, she had her wish to have me all to herself. I was with her most of what was to be her last day at home. I had taken Sarah for a swimming lesson after school and had then been home to see to the family. I returned in the evening to find Mummy lying on the floor beside her bed. I called the doctor who called an ambulance. On admission to the Royal Infirmary, an x-ray revealed that Mummy had sustained a fractured femur. I just knew when the ambulance men carried her out of the house that she would never return to her own home and that day was to be the last time that I had a normal conversation with her.

Eventually, Mummy's admission into a new unit at Astley Ainslie hospital instead of the psychiatric one was such a relief. Astley Ainslie has lovely grounds where I could take her for walks in a wheelchair. Mummy's cognitive condition had become much worse probably due to the anaesthetic when she had surgery for her fractured femur. When I brought her to our house on her birthday, she obviously did not recognise it and said, 'How long have you lived here?' I think that on occasions she thought that I was Auntie Lah as she would ask what father was doing today and when Sarah was with me she would say, 'I see you've brought little Esther with you today.'

I had often regretted that I let Mummy move, but over the years I have seen that it was best for her. Mummy being a very private person would not have liked local people at home to see her as she was at the end of her life. The care of Mummy was of an extremely high standard. God certainly made the transition from being at home to being in care easy for her and I will always be thankful for that.

Our children spent many hours of their childhood in hospitals but this has not deterred either of them from pursuing careers in caring professions; in fact, it actively encouraged Sarah.

The beginning of December arrived and with it my birthday. I wondered what this birthday would bring – I was soon to find out. During the afternoon one of Mummy's neighbours telephoned to say she thought that Mummy's house had been broken into. I went, and sure enough, someone had entered via a window on the side of the house. The burglar had fled having been disturbed by a light coming on, and had taken only a few possessions.

Approximately three weeks later on the morning of Christmas Eve, I was making mince pies when another of Mummy's neighbours telephoned, saying that there appeared to be a problem with Mummy's house. I went and the neighbour's husband met me at the door. The windows were totally steamed up. We entered and it was like going into a sauna! The water main in the attic had burst. One side of the house was completely sodden; all we could do was turn the water and electricity off. Addie was working, but soon arrived at the house having bought an aqua-vac en route. I worked in wellingtons with my anorak hood up as the water was still coming through the ceiling and light fittings! The dishes in the sideboard were full of water! I would not wish this on anyone. It was awful. We could only work until daylight faded, and then had to leave things as they were until after Boxing Day, when businesses, necessary for the clearing up, reopened after the holiday. Auntie Jean was staying with us and we were also able to bring Mummy and Granny out of their respective hospitals to spend Christmas day with us on what was probably one of our most bizarre Christmas days.

A year after Mummy's fall, knowing that there was no possibility of her ever returning home, and after all the calamities that had befallen it, we decided to sell the house. Once more, I began sorting, clearing and packing.

When going through Mummy's desk I found three pieces of paper. One was a typed letter on official headed notepaper from the Mission of Hope, Rescue Maternity Hospital, Children's Homes, and Registered Adoption Society. The address was 'Birdhurst Lodge,' South Park Hill Road, Croydon, Surrey. Wow!

The letter was a reply to one sent by Mummy less than three weeks after bringing me home to Seahouses. She had been asking how long it would be before wee Esther would become their own. The last two paragraphs of the reply read as follows:

'To come back to your precious little daughter, it is lovely to know that she is getting on so well and I rejoice to see that you can speak of her as having made home "HOME" to you in the true sense of the word. May she continue to bring much joy to you and may you early have the privilege of leading her to the Saviour.'

What a discovery! I had not been born in London so I was no Cockney! Of course, my parents had to go to Croydon via King's Cross, hence the tale of the man carrying me on the escalator.

Down the side of the notepaper was a list of the president and several vice presidents of the mission, and amongst those names was the person that Auntie Martin knew, the Princess Despina.

On the second very flimsy piece of paper there was a handwritten list with my name, Noelle, born December 1943, birth weight 5lb 14oz, present weight 8lb 4oz. It then went on to list my feeds. Next was the all-important registration of my ration books to retailers in Croydon and Blackfriars SE1.

The third piece of paper was a very official form. It was the court Adoption Order, dated the 9th August 1944, in respect of an infant named Esther Elizabeth, formerly Noelle... further down the form it stated that she was the child of Grace Violet...

Well! I now had the name of my birth mother and from that time on the names Grace Violet have always been in my mind and I have always thought of her with both names. Once more, I wondered what she was like. What did she look like? Did she ever think about me? Had she ever wondered about whether she might have grandchildren somewhere?

13

Death and Illness

DURING THE SUMMER of 1986 we very sadly said goodbye to Auntie Jean who died after a short stay in hospital, leaving us once more with a large gap in our family life. She had increasingly been our active, older family member admirably filling the role of substitute grandmother, teaching Sarah to knit and always being interested in whatever sport Christopher was currently focusing on. I wish I had asked her more questions about my adoptive family. However, she did share many family stories with me, telling me things about Daddy that I had not previously known and some secrets surrounding the wider family.

I had sometimes remarked to Addie that in all probability, our mothers might die within a short time of each other and this proved to be the case. During the course of Mummy's hospitalisation, the hospital had sent for me several times when her condition deteriorated but she had always rallied. Each time I had prayed and had almost as it were willed her to live; I was not yet ready for her to leave me even though she was no longer aware of my presence; until her birthday in August 1987 – having taken a birthday cake which she could no longer eat, a birthday present she was not aware of and which I opened on my own. I returned to the car and wept. How much more could I take? Thankfully, I was able to spend a lot of time with her in the last few days of her life and was there when she finally passed away in November 1987 aged 88 years. I was finally willing to let her go and as I sat beside her bedside I was singing to myself the hymn 'O love that will not let me go' written by George Matheson and this was one of the hymns that we sang at her funeral.

We took Mummy back to Seahouses and laid her to rest beside Daddy, in the cemetery at North Sunderland. Prior to this Mummy's funeral service was held in the Methodist Chapel, Seahouses, where she had previously worshipped for so many years. It was as she had predicted her only and final return to Seahouses, but we knew that she was safe with her Lord and Saviour and that one day we will be with her again.

Ten weeks later in February 1988 Granny passed away after eleven long frustrating years in hospital and as with Mummy, we were comforted to know that one day we will see her again.

The year 1988 was to be a turbulent year for our family, with all four of us having health problems – Christopher with a virus that seemed to go on for months, Sarah suffering from a prolapsed disc in her spine, Addie being diagnosed with asthma and myself who needed minor surgery, plus the death of Addie's brother-in-law towards the end of the year. We did manage a holiday that we had booked in the spring prior to Sarah having her back problem. Because she could not sit for any length of time we resorted to travelling on the motor rail service to King's Cross station, London, and then by car to Canterbury. Addie and Christopher went on excursions especially to cricket matches while Sarah and I made one or two visits to a chiropractor in Canterbury! However, Sarah did manage a few short outings but most of the time she lay on the sofa and became an enduring fan of the Tour de France, watching it on television each day at our holiday house located in an old Oast House.

We were delighted and so very thankful that both Christopher and Sarah committed their lives to Jesus Christ as teenagers and subsequently asked to be baptised. When they were babies, we had held a short service in our home to dedicate them to the Lord. This was instead of having them baptised, the belief of the Old Schoolhouse Christian Fellowship being that of believers' baptism, that is to say an individual is baptised after they accept Jesus Christ as their Saviour.

In April 1990, Christopher celebrated his twenty-first birthday, the actual day being on a Saturday. He chose to spend the day watching the annual Melrose rugby sevens in the Scottish Borders, in the pouring rain I might add. Addie and Sarah braved the elements with him but I stayed at home with Jasper!

Jasper had increasing health problems, which finally took him from us at the end of January 1991 after twelve years as a wonderful doggie companion. This was a year of milestones in the family with Christopher graduating from university in Edinburgh and Sarah leaving school and preparing to go to Aberdeen to study. Addie and I were now facing the possibility of having no one at home. However, Christopher was to stay at home for another two years.

Now I had spare time which was something of a novelty for me and I was wondering what I might do with it. One day a friend invited me to go with her to the National Bible Society for Scotland, to find out about a project called Bible World for which they were requiring volunteers. We went along and came away with us both having volunteered. The aim of Bible World was to explain how the Bible had come to us down through the centuries to its present form. The project had been set up to complement the religious education syllabus in schools from mid-primary school to second year senior school. It had been extremely well planned and the children thoroughly enjoyed their experience. Those who visited were able to feel paper made from papyrus, dress up as monks and make a copy of the Lord's Prayer using a printing press. They also played biblical games on computers and then went through passport control before boarding a mock spaceship for a flight taking them back to first century earth to find Jesus of Nazareth.

All of this was very stimulating with lots of fun for both children and volunteers. This new venture in my life certainly took me out of my comfort zone, as I had to learn about computers and listen to the sound of my own voice when talking to the children. These were things that I had never done previously. I loved volunteering at Bible World, it was such a rewarding experience and I count it a privilege to have been able to work there for eleven years.

Our silver wedding celebration in 1992 saw Addie and I having a short break at a delightful hotel on the shores of the Lake of Menteith. Later we celebrated with the family when we had lunch in a local hotel in Edinburgh. Then it was back home for tea and a showing of our wedding cine film which Addie had surprised me with, having had it put onto a video; it was quite an emotional experience seeing so many people no longer with us. How thankful we were to the Lord for all the blessings he had bestowed upon us in our twenty-five years of marriage.

This was also to be the year of my first flight, which was to Lanzarote. I couldn't understand why Addie and Sarah, who were going on holiday with me, abandoned me on the steps of the plane. They went ahead and disappeared inside and I was left standing at the bottom of the steps waiting to board. When I arrived at our seat, they promptly told me I must sit between them – all very odd! It wasn't until we arrived back home that Christopher informed me that Addie and Sarah expected me to chicken out of my first flight knowing as they did my fear of flying over deep water.

My second flight followed the next year as we headed to America for a whole month! Addie and I joined Sarah after she finished working in one of the American camps for schoolchildren. Christopher came for part of the time and after returning to Edinburgh, he moved into his first flat, which he had bought a few weeks earlier. Now Addie and I were definitely on our own.

Sarah chose to celebrate her twenty-first birthday in true Scottish style by having a ceilidh for family and friends during the Easter holidays of 1994, prior to her going off to Barnsley to do a university placement. After graduating, she returned to Barnsley where she took up a temporary post but was soon to move even further south to a permanent post in Leicester. Now both children had truly flown the nest and Addie who had been contemplating retirement for a while decided to make definite plans.

In September, we went to Dublin for a few nights. Soon after arriving, we received a telephone call from Christopher to say that he had broken his leg. Christopher at this stage was the leader of the young people at Charlotte Baptist Chapel in Edinburgh. The accident happened while on a weekend away with this group. Christopher told us not to worry, he was fine and that he had returned to our home, to a ground floor bedroom and a friend would stay with him until we came home. On returning home, we discovered that the broken leg had needed surgery, with a plate and several pins inserted and then put into plaster. He had also required stiches to a cut on his head. This all happened because a doorway in the centre where they were staying was an illegal height; Christopher had gone through the doorway, hitting his head as he went. This caused him to go over on his ankle, which fractured and spiralled up the fibula. All was well until the first plaster change after which Christopher became very unwell.

The next weeks were some of the worst in our lives when Christopher developed a large blood clot in his leg with smaller ones ending up in his lungs. Eventually he was admitted to hospital, by which time he had double pneumonia. I returned home for a short while before returning with Addie at visiting time when we were told that Christopher's condition had worsened and that he was about to be moved to the high dependency unit. When I said to the doctor that I was glad that Christopher was in the right place, she replied, 'I don't know about that, I think it is more a case of divine intervention being required.' Not what one normally hears from doctors? We of course had been praying about Christopher's condition but now things were apparently very much worse. I acted on the doctor's information and went straight to the telephone.

It was a Thursday evening, the night our Fellowship house groups met. I telephoned one of the leaders asking them to pray and asked that he tell the other house groups. I then telephoned the Charlotte Chapel elder connected with the youth work at the Chapel.The elder happened to be a doctor and was a marvellous support to us, coming immediately to the hospital. It was wonderful to have so many people in our Fellowship and at Charlotte Chapel and indeed all around the country praying for Christopher and for us as a family.

I sat that night by my son's bedside watching him suffer, not knowing whether he would live or die and like the majority of parents who find themselves in that position wishing that it was me and not Christopher in that hospital bed.

I am thankful to say that Christopher made a good recovery albeit with permanent vascular damage to his leg. Many times since that night, I have thought about that experience and have found myself drawing a comparison of how God had wonderfully spared us our son, but had in fact sent to earth his one and only son Jesus, knowing that He had to die. Jesus died a horrendous death when crucified in order to take the punishment for my sin by the shedding of His blood. This was God's plan for the salvation of those who put their trust in Jesus and accept Him as their saviour. How wonderfully merciful God is to all who put their trust in Him and how amazing is His Grace by giving us what we don't deserve. All this in spite of my many faults and failings, is incredible; in fact, there are no suitable adjectives to describe the mercy and grace of God. How thankful I am that God sent his son Jesus to pay the price for my sin and that I decided to accept him as my saviour.

Shortly before Addie's retirement in April 1996, I became unwell. The doctor put it down to stress which had built up over the preceding months and my life was about to undergo another big change; retirement for one spouse means change for both, especially if one has been at home on their own for much of the time and in control of the daily routine. I was glad that I was able to go to Addie's office and attend his retirement celebrations and to a special dinner for his close colleagues. Addie chose to retire on a Thursday and the next morning he asked me if I would like breakfast in bed at some unearthly hour! I said no thank you!

A few weeks later at the beginning of May, we set off for a short holiday in Wales, which was what we both needed and really enjoyed. We stayed in the heart of the countryside and I can remember thinking how good it was to be alive and what a wonderful Creator God we have. We had some lovely walks in the Elan valley and my lasting memory of that holiday is of the hedges swathed in frothy blackthorn blossom and of the peace and quiet with just birdsong to be heard; a wonderful start to Addie's retirement.

In May 1997 we had a short break in Paris to celebrate our thirtieth wedding anniversary. This was to be my first time in Paris. Taking Eurostar from Ashford in Kent, it proved to be very enjoyable apart from my continuous back pain meaning many painkillers were required to cope with the amount of walking. We stayed in Ashford before and after our trip and once again admired the Kent countryside and vowed to return sometime in the future. We did not envisage how soon our return was to be. Only three months later we found ourselves helping Sarah relocate from Leicester to Canterbury where she had obtained a new post. This was to be the first of many enjoyable visits to Kent staying in bed and breakfast accommodation or a cottage close to the oast house where we had stayed nine years previously.

After the death of Mummy, Christopher had said to me that if I ever wanted to look for my birth mother he was willing to help me. My reply was no. I also heard or read about an agency that could assist you in finding your birth relatives but although I was curious, I still had the feeling of being disloyal to my adoptive parents whom I loved dearly. There was also the fear of possible rejection.

With Sarah living in Kent, I did at times wonder if she might have a grandmother living somewhere near, seeing I had been born in the next county of Surrey; but then I would dismiss the thoughts from my mind. I had recurring thoughts about Grace Violet being my own flesh and blood and like me she had need of a Saviour and that I should look for her so that I could share with her the good news about Jesus just in case she was not already aware of it. Sadly, I did nothing.

14

Freedom to Travel

ADDIE'S RETIREMENT meant that we were able to travel. We enjoyed holidays in many parts of the world and of course our own, much loved country. One memorable holiday comes to mind but not for the right reasons. We were holidaying in Devon in 1998. After enjoying a meal with a friend, we set off to return to our holiday home. It was late at night. Our friend's house had a shared drive, accessed by a cattle grid. It was very dark with no street lighting. I was guiding Addie out as he reversed the car onto a main road. In the darkness, I forgot about the cattle grid and fell through it! As I tried to extricate myself, I looked around and saw the car reversing towards me! Newspaper headlines flashed through my mind: 'Husband reverses car over wife stuck in cattle grid!' I got out partially, but fell a second time. Mercifully, Addie saw me go down this time, stopped, and came to my rescue. We continued with our holiday but I returned home with a broken wrist, proof of my adventure.

The year 2000 dawned and with it an opportunity to visit Israel and Jordan. We flew to Gatwick where we met up with the tour leader and the rest of the group. We soon became part of it and are still in touch with some of the friends we made.

We started the tour in Jerusalem later going to Bethlehem, Bethany and the Mount of Olives. We then went to Gethsemane and the Garden Tomb followed by the Shrine of the Book and the Holocaust museum. How amazing it was to walk where Jesus walked. The Bible certainly came alive. Our journey took us next to Jericho to see some of the brick walls that Joshua brought tumbling down! On through the desert we went, to Qumran. The discovery of the Dead Sea Scrolls was in the caves at Qumran and visiting the site was special for me as we had a board in Bible World explaining to the children how the scrolls authenticate the book of Isaiah, written thousands of years ago. This proves the accuracy of the scribes long ago and the translators of today's Bible.

On we went, stopping at Masada and ascending by cable car to the summer palace built by Herod, all quite incredible. Later on that day Addie went for a float in the Dead Sea. I refrained but did test the water with my hand, ugh! It felt very oily and I was glad I had not ventured in.

After an overnight stop at Arad we continued through the desert to the border crossing point near Eilat where we would cross into Jordan. We left our Israeli coach and proceeded to transport our own luggage through no man's land to the Jordanian border and there we experienced trouble. After the searching of our bags, all food was confiscated. This was our lunch! Eventually common sense prevailed with the officials allowing us to eat it in the customs building. We boarded the coach along with our Jordanian tour guide plus two armed police officers!

Leaving the Red Sea behind, our journey continued through the desert on the Jordanian side of the Dead Sea arriving at Petra late at night. Having been wakened at some unearthly hour by the local Imam calling the faithful to prayer, meant we had no difficulty in being ready for our early start into old Petra. We walked in and the gradual revelation of the treasury was quite stunning. It is well described as being 'rose red'.

The next day after another early start, we were back on the desert road. Realising that we were following in the footsteps of Moses as he led the Children of Israel from Egypt to the Promised Land, I now hold this prophet in high regard. What a journey that must have been, all those thousands of people and animals. We eventually reached Mount Nebo and like Moses stood looking towards Jericho viewing the Promised Land. My keepsake from

Mount Nebo is a glass Christmas tree ornament that comes out every year.

Amman was our overnight stop. We did not have time to see much but I will never forget the bed we slept on. I think the mattress must have been made of concrete. I even managed to graze my knee on it. Visiting the Roman city of Jerash was an altogether different experience but quite fascinating. Leaving Jerash behind we drove past the Jabbok River, (where Jacob wrestled with God) to the border crossing. We went over the river Jordan back into Israel at the Allenby Bridge. We encountered more problems with border guards. We did not know that we were required to pay to leave the country so a mad search for cash ensued, only to have our Scottish bank notes returned! Fortunately, our fellow travellers who were mostly English managed to rake up and lend us the required amount of cash! I remember feeling very disappointed when discovering that the river Jordan was only a large ditch at the crossing point.

Back to Israel and to our lovely Israeli tourist guide who was a Palestinian Christian. Our time was nearly over ending with a final two-night stay in Tiberias, which meant we were able to visit Nazareth and Capernaum from where we sailed across the Sea of Galilee. The final evening we visited a diamond factory and managed to refrain from buying! We did have an interesting conversation with one of the salesmen who just happened to come from Dumfries, back home in Scotland and had gone to school with a friend of Christopher's. A small world! The day of departure took us to Meggido, Mount Carmel, and Ceasarea Maritima, then on to Tel Aviv airport.

It had been a never to be forgotten holiday and one which encouraged me very much in my Christian faith.

Later during the summer of 2000, Christopher brought a young lady called Janet to have Sunday lunch with us. This was the first of many visits by Janet culminating with her parents and sister having lunch with us on Hogmanay. As they left, they very kindly invited us to have Sunday lunch with them at their home in Perthshire, the date being confirmed later. The night prior to our visit to Perthshire, Christopher telephoned and said, 'Mum, you might like to take your camera with you tomorrow.' Well! This suggestion could mean only one thing. An engagement must be imminent! Christopher collected us, and then Janet. She got in the car but there was no sign of an engagement ring. We had to wait until after morning service, and lunch, before Christopher announced the news that we were anticipating. Christopher had made a secret journey to ask Janet's parents for her hand in marriage and had only proposed to Janet the previous evening. He had already bought the engagement ring; that is what I call brave! This news sparked wedding fever. A date in November having been decided upon, all the planning then commenced.

During the spring, Addie and I managed visits to Canterbury and Copenhagen. Whilst in Copenhagen I had real mobility problems with my back and hip. I was becoming increasingly lame and later in the summer I was finally diagnosed with an arthritic hip and referred to a consultant. Shortly after the engagement, Christopher came back to live at home having sold his flat, he and Janet having decided to start married life in Janet's flat. Now I was back to catering and caring for three. Addie and I had a brief respite from all the activity when we had a mini visit to Anglesey to see friends of Addie's from his R.A.F. days when stationed at Valley.

The first weekend in September I achieved one of my 'must do' things – a visit to Lords cricket ground to see a match. Christopher and Addie had for many years gone to the Nat. West final and that year Christopher was unable to attend, so my big chance came and I made the most of it. Sarah came up to London from Canterbury and we had one day looking for wedding outfits, which was great fun but also frustrating! However, Sarah was planning a visit home later in the month so we still had time to complete our search.

I have vivid memories of 9/11. I was at Bible World that morning and on arriving home, I found Addie watching on television the horrific events that were taking place in America. That evening it was our Ladies Fellowship; before going out I sat at the piano and played 'Be still and know that I am God' which is in verse 10 of Psalm 46. I went to the Ladies Fellowship and the speaker said, 'Before we start can we sing "Be still and know that I am God".' A week or two later a gentleman who had been on holiday in Spain at the time said that on hearing the awful news he immediately thought of 'Be still and know that I am God.' How amazing that we all wanted to remember that God is always in control however bad things might be. Two days later, Sarah flew home amid much airport security. The following day while out shopping in Jenners department store, Sarah and I stood for the two minutes silence to remember the victims of 9/11. An experience I will never forget.

The wedding date drew nearer with mounting excitement. A pleasant late November day heralded the much anticipated occasion. Having stayed overnight at the hotel where the reception was to be held, we enjoyed a relaxing morning before getting ready for the wedding. The wedding service was at 3pm and we emerged from the church as darkness fell. The light shining from the church windows was so effective and reminded me of how Jesus Christ the Light of The World shines out into the darkness of this world.

What a year 2001 had been and it ended with having Janet with us for the first time on Christmas Day, when we also welcomed one of Daddy's youngest cousins to stay with us, as it was to be her first Christmas on her own. We now had two people to initiate into the customs of the Harkess household at Christmas, so like those of 'Romany' days but now the traditions began to change but in a pleasant way.

15

Operations and Accidents

IN MARCH 2002 I saw the orthopaedic consultant who confirmed that I did need a hip replacement and wanted to put me straight onto the waiting list. This came as rather a shock as I thought I was too young, so he agreed to see me the following year unless I decided I could no longer wait!

Sarah had decided to leave Canterbury and we helped her move back home that Easter. Moving Sarah is no mean feat as she has a habit of collecting many things and this time was no exception. Our two cars were full to overflowing and we had to engage the services of a haulage firm to bring a pallet north! The pallet arrived in Edinburgh before us!

After a few weeks, Sarah left to take up a temporary post in the north east of Scotland returning home later in the summer before taking up a permanent post in County Durham.

Our celebration that year was Addie's seventieth birthday. He eventually agreed to the planning of a small party for his family and some close friends and he actually enjoyed it!

Addie had been treated for asthma for the previous fifteen years. Sarah had noticed that our G.P. practice ran an asthma clinic and said, 'Dad, why have you never been to the asthma clinic?' 'I just get my repeat prescription,' Addie replied, but this conversation prompted him to attend the clinic. The clinic nurse suspected that he did not have asthma and referred him to a G.P. who in turn referred him to a cardiologist. We came away from that appointment with an angiogram scheduled for the beginning of December. At that point, I prayed that if there was something wrong that there would be suitable treatment.

December came and following the angiogram Addie telephoned from the hospital to say I could collect him, but not to come until 5pm as the cardiologist wanted to speak to both of us. I knew then that all was not well. The cardiologist confirmed that Addie needed a triple coronary artery bypass, and he was going onto the waiting list immediately. This was a shock! How thankful we were that treatment was available. Addie was told to take life easily until the operation.

Shortly after Addie's diagnoses we went house hunting with Sarah and were so relieved that she had an offer for a house accepted straight away. The entry date was the middle of January! Christmas that year was enjoyable but we made it easy.

In the middle of January 2003, Addie and I packed the car with many of Sarah's possessions and headed for County Durham, having booked into a hotel for a few nights. Moving day for Sarah was as expected, quite traumatic! Sarah's move from Leicester to Canterbury had been during a heat wave, and this move was to be the reverse, in a blizzard! There were two cars full of belongings with Addie unable to lift anything heavy. Sarah and I were slipping and sliding as we unloaded the cars but eventually we made it and Sarah slept that night on an inflatable mattress on the floor. The purchasing of a bed was then her first priority!

About six weeks later at the beginning of March, Christopher, Janet, Sarah and I all visited Addie in hospital the evening before his bypass operation. We left him confident in the knowledge that he was in God's hands whatever the outcome. Just before going to bed I went into the study to replace a book. On the desk was an envelope, addressed to Christopher and Sarah in case we should require the contents. I burst into tears. I had coped for nearly six months and finally everything caught up with me. Sarah heard me and when seeing the envelope said very defiantly, 'It's alright, Dad's coming home and then we'll tear it up.' I went to bed. On my pillow was a piece of paper. Written in Addie's handwriting were four Bible references for me to look up.

Joshua ch.1 v 9: 'Have I not commanded you? Be strong and courageous. Do not be terrified; do not be discouraged, for the Lord your God will be with you wherever you go.'

Psalm 27 v 14: 'Wait for the Lord; be strong and take heart and wait for the Lord.'

Isaiah ch. 26 v 3: 'You will keep him in perfect peace, him whose mind is steadfast, because he trusts in you.'

Zephaniah ch. 3 v 17: 'The Lord your God is with you, he is mighty to save. He will take great delight in you, he will quiet you with his love, he will rejoice over you with singing.'

What amazing words of comfort. Lovingly put before me when I most needed them by my wonderful husband. I went to bed and slept.

Operation day dawned and we had a telephone call from Addie shortly before going to the operating theatre. There was a great sense of peace. Sarah and I decided to go out for the morning and taking a mobile phone with us, we headed for Marks and Spencer at The Gyle shopping mall, returning home at lunchtime when Janet joined us. I kept busy during the afternoon and prepared a meal for the four of us to have together that evening. When telephoning the hospital at teatime the news was good – Addie's operation had gone well, he was out of theatre, now in the intensive care unit and we would be able to visit the next day. How relieved and thankful we were, but it was only the beginning of what seemed a long and frustrating road to recovery.

Addie made good progress and was able to come home on the sixth day after his operation but a week later, his heart went into fibrillation. His readmittance to hospital was necessary and he had a cardio version procedure done the next day. It was the first of three readmissions to hospital within four weeks of his operation. He told me later that on the second readmission he really thought he was going to die when being treated in the resuss room. These readmissions were during the night. I became very adept at dressing quickly and going without socks as I hurried to go with him!

I remember distinctly being brought home in a taxi about four o'clock in the morning by an extremely kind taxi driver who declined a tip as he never took them from people coming from the hospital. As I put my key in the door, I was very aware of the presence of the Lord and not being afraid at all.

The day after Addie's discharge from hospital, I had a consultation with the orthopaedic surgeon who understood my current position; this led to having my surgery delayed again.

Battling with embolism stockings was very difficult for me; my back did not appreciate all the bending. That situation was taken care of with the prescribing of warfarin, meaning that Addie was no longer required to wear them. I heaved a sigh of relief!

During one of his stays in hospital, Addie unfortunately acquired M.R.S.A. in all three of his wounds, which took about four months to heal. I would not wish this on anyone. All these things added to the normal psychological trauma that can occur after bypass surgery; it meant that sometimes we would end up in tears together.

Addie's first outing apart from hospital visits was to view a property that Christopher and Janet were interested in buying, which they subsequently went on to purchase. Addie was very frustrated not being able to help with the removal. However, I was of some use as they had no washing machine for several weeks after moving and I was able to provide the services of a launderette!

August saw Addie having to have another cardio version, after which he really started to improve, and he, Sarah and I were able to enjoy a week's holiday in the southern Lake District. Life appeared to be returning to normal. Not quite! Sarah had a bad car accident at the beginning of December as she was coming home to celebrate my sixtieth birthday. Mercifully, she was unharmed. The car was a write off! It was the end of a traumatic year.

I felt I could not face surgery in 2004 and my GP thought likewise, so once again I saw the rescheduling of my hip replacement. Finally, at the end of January 2005, my surgery took place. It was a success. Right from the beginning, my walking was excellent and I continued to improve throughout the summer, enjoying a holiday beside Loch Awe where we rediscovered the area. I certainly benefited from my hip replacement and continued to improve.

In the spring of 2006 Daddy's cousin was unwell and had several hospital appointments. She decided to have me accompany her so our time spent in Northumberland was considerable. Several times she said to me, 'You are very like your maternal grandmother.' Did she not know of my adoption? I decided to inquire when she next mentioned the subject, which of course she did. I said to her, 'You do know that I was adopted?' 'Yes,' she replied, 'but that makes no difference and you do look like your grandmother.' She would never know what those words meant to me. Not having known my grandmother I couldn't comment. According to those that did know her, she was a warm, loving and very hospitable lady, and someone I would have wanted to take after.

Operations behind us, Addie and I felt confident enough to go abroad, to Ibizia, much to Sarah's amusement as she thought we must be going to go clubbing! The holiday was a success – we walked and travelled on the local buses, which meant us having to negotiate a very steep hill on returning to our holiday home. I was glad I had packed my folding walking stick! Addie was in the seventh heaven with all the amazing sunsets for him to photograph.

July presented me with the opportunity of accomplishing another of my 'must do' things. It was my first visit to Wimbledon. Sarah had encouraged me to apply for tickets and I had the good fortune to be allocated two, which meant that Sarah could accompany me. Being a seasoned Wimbledon goer Sarah knew all the short cuts and I thoroughly enjoyed the experience.

Towards the end of the year I returned to Northumberland for two weeks to care for Daddy's cousin who eventually had to have an operation. Thankfully, this was a success and Sarah was able to collect her and bring her to Edinburgh for Christmas.

Forty years: could it possibly be that long since that very special day in April 1967? The question was how to celebrate this special event in 2007. After much thought and family dialogue, we decided to have a family weekend in Barcelona. None of us had been there so we could discover the delights of the city together. This we did, with all five of us flying from Edinburgh. Barcelona is an amazing city, the architecture being unique and we made the most of our visit.

Celebrating our ruby wedding in Barcelona

Later on, we invited Addie's family to lunch in a favourite restaurant and then to our home for afternoon tea complete with Ruby Wedding cake. In August Addie, Sarah and I spent a few days with Daddy's cousin in Northumberland hearing yet more family stories!

October saw us returning to Bassenfell Manor, a Christian outdoor Centre in the northern Lake District, where we had been going to a house party every October since 2000. As before, we really enjoyed meeting up with old and new friends and hearing more of God's word from the Bible.

Daddy's cousin came to spend Christmas with us as usual, with Christopher and Janet coming for Christmas dinner. They left about 5pm to go and spend the evening with Janet's family in Perthshire. We settled down for a relaxing evening, telephoning Addie's family and me playing with my new camera, a Christmas present from the family. The telephone rang several times that evening but nobody replied when I answered. At last, someone did reply. It was Christopher. 'Mum, we've had a car accident and we're in A & E.' I said, 'Which hospital?' He replied, 'The Royal Infirmary.' I thought it must be the one in Perth but 'No' was the reply when I asked again. The accident had happened on the Edinburgh city bypass shortly after leaving our house.

Christopher asked us to collect clothes as what they had been wearing had been cut off by the paramedics. Addie and I set off and I shall never forget the sight of them when reaching A & E. There they were, lying on trolleys, side by side, sucking lollipops given to them by the staff. It would have been very funny if it were not so serious. They were very shocked and traumatised but having sustained only minor injuries were soon able to go home, and Sarah stayed overnight with them. How fortunate they had been. One of the nurses in A & E had passed the accident on her way to work, and presumed that there would be no survivors so was utterly amazed when discovering that all those involved were walking wounded. Christopher was not to blame – the other driver accepted responsibility.

Early 2008 my orthopaedic surgeon referred me for a walking test to ascertain whether my other hip would benefit from replacement. The test showed that surgery would indeed be of benefit to me so onto another waiting list I went.

In March 2008, Daddy's cousin suffered a severe stroke and again we spent a considerable amount of time in Northumberland, which we loved to do, but not under those circumstances. Sadly, she died after ten weeks in hospital but I was very privileged to be with her at the end of her very long and interesting life. Another large gap left in our lives with her passing.

16

Looking for Grace

SARAH, being our family historian, has worked on the family trees on both sides of the family, in some instances tracing relatives centuries back.

During the summer of 2008 I asked Sarah to put my birth name into the search engine of the ancestry website that she uses, to see what we could discover. I had imagined my birth mother Grace to be very young when I was born and that she would have probably been unmarried.

Sarah discovered that I was the only baby born in England in 1943 with my name. Grace's maiden name was found and that of her mother and they appeared to come from Essex. Interestingly we discovered that Grace was married when she gave birth to me, so I wondered why she had given me away. Perhaps her husband was not my father or she may have become a widow and been unable to care for me by herself. Whatever the reason something had caused her to part with me. However, I now had a snippet of information as to where my natural roots lay.

A few weeks later Addie and I were once more back for our annual October week at Bassenfell Manor. During the course of our time there, I had a conversation with Audrey (the speaker's wife). We talked about when a person accepts the Lord Jesus as their Saviour, that they are as it were adopted into God's family. I found myself saying, 'Not every Christian can say that they have been adopted twice.' 'Oh, were you adopted?' asked Audrey. 'Yes,' I said and explained that I had been born in Croydon at a Christian charity home called the Mission of Hope. Audrey stared at me and said, 'Birdhurst?' It was my turn to stare at her as I replied, 'Yes.' Audrey's jaw dropped as she gasped. 'My mother worked there before she was married and she used to tell us stories about the children in the children's home.' Now my jaw dropped, 'Really!' After all these years, I was now talking to somebody who actually knew something about the place where I was born!

I left Bassenfell with many thoughts about the circumstances of my birth. I was now very curious. Two lots of information in a relatively short space of time made me ask the question, 'Did I want to try to discover more?' Yes, but not quite yet.

My first priority was my next hip replacement, planned for early in the New Year. Unfortunately, there was a delay until the end of March due to me having M.R.S.A.in my throat. My recovery was much slower than the first time. Much patience was required. I watched more television than usual – one programme being the current series of 'Who do you think you are?' So many of the people who took part in those programmes discovered horrendous things about their forebears, but they seemed to cope with the information. I thought of how I might feel if faced with similar revelations.

I had of course at times wondered who my father might have been and can remember thinking on Remembrance Sundays that maybe my father had been one of the many who died during the Second World War. I also considered the possibility that I was illegitimate, which in those days was a very shameful thing for the mother to bear. There was also a stigma attached to the child; even after adoption people tended to presume, unless knowing otherwise, that the child had been illegitimate.

I know that the changing attitudes of society have made it much easier for people like me to talk about the circumstances of their birth. So many women suffered appalling treatment when requiring love and compassion.

Another situation that an adoptee has to face and I had never given it any thought until I considered searching, was that there was the possibility that I might have been the result of rape. How would I feel about that? Horrified might be a good description; and yet, I still wanted to know where my roots lay. These are some of the thoughts which probably go through the minds of innumerable people weighing up the pros and cons of starting to search for their birth parents. That was it. I decided to stop imagining and find out about the other me. There was only one thing to do. I must search for more information. How could I do this? I guessed that obtaining my original birth certificate would be a good place to start.

In August 2009 I telephoned Sarah and asked her to order my original birth certificate, also the marriage certificate of Grace and her husband Eric. This would tell us where their marriage took place and their occupations.

Moments later, the telephone rang. Sarah's voice said, 'Mum, before sending for the certificates I put Eric's name into the Ancestry website instead of yours or Grace's and somebody has put Grace's family tree onto the website.' I said, 'Oh why did that not show before?' Sarah replied, 'Because it was the first time I had entered Eric's name. Eric died in 1950 but they had a son. I don't know his first name but his wife was called Gillian and she died a few years ago. They appear to have two daughters but I don't know their names.' My head was beginning to reel! Sarah carried on. 'Mum, Grace remarried in 1953 and had three more children but her second husband, Richard, died in 1968, and when I click on Grace's name it says information withheld, person still living.' I said, 'What! Grace is still alive!'

I then said, 'What will we do now?' I will never forget the vehement reply that ensued as Sarah's voice came down the phone: 'Nothing, she's not family.' I was devastated. I replied, 'Well Sarah, if it hadn't been for Grace I wouldn't be here. Christopher wouldn't be here. You wouldn't be here. Dad wouldn't have the wife he has. Janet wouldn't have the husband she has. So we all have something to thank Grace for.' I know that God gave me those words to say. I did not have time to think of them. Sarah continued, 'Mum, you don't need to worry about her, she's not some little old lady with no one to care about her. She has a family.'

I said no more, apart from asking for the purchase of the birth and marriage certificates to go ahead. I knew that I could go no further unless Sarah changed her attitude. The only way this was going to happen was to take it to the Lord in prayer. I once again heeded the favourite quotation of Mummy: 'More things are wrought by prayer than this world dreams of.'

I prayed.

The certificates arrived in due course. My birth certificate was as expected, with no father named. Grace's marriage certificate showed that she had been married at the beginning of November 1939 in Romford and that her husband Eric had been a police constable in Romford. I felt we could discover so much more, but I must have patience I told myself. Grace if still living would be eighty-eight years old so time was of the essence.

At the beginning of October, Addie and I again went for our annual week at Bassenfell Manor. Audrey was there and I had so much to tell her. After informing her of everything, she said, 'What are you going to do?' I explained that I could not proceed further without my daughter's blessing. Audrey immediately replied, 'Don't you think that Grace would want to know that you have been alright?' Yes, being a mother myself I had to agree.

I know that God has intervened in my life in the past and has plans for my future. As it says in Ephesians ch3 v20: 'Now to him who is able to do immeasurably more than all we ask or imagine, according to his power that is at work within us.' I was quietly confident.

I told my story to someone else staying at the Manor, who had earlier lived in Croydon for many years. She told me that the Mission of Hope had still been in existence when she lived in Croydon and that the children who lived in their children's home went to a Sunday school at a certain mission hall.

17

Biblical Lessons

AFTER LEAVING Bassenfell, we crossed over to the north east of the country to spend the weekend with Sarah. Later on that evening, Sarah showed me on her computer all the information she had found. She clicked on Grace's name and the words 'information withheld, person still living' came up. My reaction to this was to say to Addie that it certainly looked as though Grace was still alive. Addie responded by saying, 'Well, what are you going to do?' Sarah's very prompt reply was, 'Dad, Mum can't just land on her doorstep and say hi, I'm Noelle!' Addie said, 'Of course she can't. Whatever happens we would have to find her first.' Another prompt reply from Sarah: 'Well, how are we going to do that?' At that moment, I knew that Sarah's attitude had changed and I silently said, 'Thank you Lord.'

Over supper we discussed the best way to proceed and decided that Sarah should email the person that had put the family tree onto the website. This would be to enquire as to whether she had any information about a Noelle... born in Croydon in 1943.

When Sarah went back into the website to find the email address, she announced, 'This was put on here in December 2000.' I looked, and could not believe my eyes when I saw the date. The 5th December 2000, my birthday! Had somebody deliberately put it on the website on that date? Sarah felt that I was reading too much into it and that it was just a coincidence. Addie kept reminding us that our coincidences are God's incidences. An email was duly written, and sent. We waited hopefully for a reply.

I prayed that if it was God's will for me to find Grace I would. If not, that the door would be very definitely closed.

When reading the story of Esther in the Bible I have always felt a bond, seeing we were both adopted, although in different ways; but I had never drawn any comparison between Joseph and me. However at this point we were studying the life of Joseph in our Sunday morning services at the Old Schoolhouse. My daily Scripture Union readings were also about Joseph. This amazing story is in Genesis chapter 37.

Knowing the story of Joseph and his removal from his birth family, albeit in a very different way to mine, I knew that God had indeed blessed Joseph, and had eventually, many years later reunited him with his family. I really felt that God was indicating that this was what he was going to do for me and that we should begin the search for Grace in earnest.

The reply to the email came after about two weeks. There was no mention of Noelle but we were able to see that this person was in fact a very distant relative of Grace.

When I asked Sarah what had changed her mind about Grace she said it was the fact that we owed our existence to Grace. Now being a very willing participant in the search, Sarah then sent for the marriage certificate of Grace's second marriage; this we felt could give us a clue as to where she might be living.

The certificate arrived showing us that Grace had married for the second time in Petersfield in Hampshire. Christopher came on board at this point and started searching electoral rolls. There were clusters of people with Grace's surname in Hampshire, Sussex and Surrey but none with the name Grace.

Prior to her second marriage Grace had been back at her parents' address and that of course was in Essex. We knew from the family tree that Grace's second husband had also died, when she was aged 46, so she may have gone back to her own part of the country, or maybe she had married again. Christopher started searching in the Essex / Suffolk area where there seemed to be groups of people with Grace's surname.

What excitement there was when Christopher announced that he had found someone called Grace, with the correct surname and in the 65-plus age bracket, living in a village on the outskirts of Saxmundham in Suffolk! I really felt that this must be Grace, but what were we to do next? I could not turn up at her door or even write a letter; she was after all an elderly lady and had a family who may not know about me.

Sarah once more came to the rescue and informed me of an organisation called Norcap who would act as mediators where a person was searching for their birth relatives. She emailed the information to Christopher who downloaded the forms and brought them to me straight away. I was so thankful that both my son and daughter had computers, as we at that stage had not dragged ourselves into the 21st century!

The forms were slightly confusing and I wanted to fill them in correctly. I telephoned Norcap for advice but there was no answer. The number was either engaged or going straight to an answer phone. I thought there might be somewhere in Edinburgh that could help me, so I telephoned our local council's social work department, but it was a Friday afternoon and it was an answer phone too. They would be back next week. How very frustrating!

Impatience was coming to the fore and I looked in the telephone directory and found a number; it was for a post adoption agency called Birthlink in Castle Street, Edinburgh. Once again, I reached for the telephone and soon a voice was asking me if they could be of any help. I said why I was telephoning and the person on the other end of the line said, 'Oh, you need the English equivalent called Norcap.' I explained that I had been trying to communicate with Norcap but had not succeeded and what I really required was some guidance on filling in the forms. 'Oh,' she said, 'one of our counsellors will be able to help you with that; I'll put you through to somebody.'

After hearing the story the next person asked, 'Where do you live?' I said, 'Here in Edinburgh' and she replied, 'That's fine, we can help you; would you like us to send out our information or would you like to have an appointment?' I immediately replied, 'I'll have an appointment please. Grace is 88 so I had better hurry up and find her.' An appointment for the following Monday afternoon ended my frustration.

18

Birthlink

THE AFTERNOON of the 2nd of November, 2009, Addie and I climbed the stairs to the Birthlink offices in Castle Street. After our introduction to Jennifer, a counsellor at Birthlink, we talked with her for about two hours. Jennifer was looking to see if I could cope with any of the situations that might arise in finding Grace.

Jennifer explained to us that Grace could have completely blanked me out of her mind and that I might face rejection. Being a mother myself, I found this very hard to believe but accepted that it might have happened. Having never felt rejection in the first instance I did not know how I would feel if this should happen now, but knew if it were to happen I would be given the strength to deal with the situation.

Jennifer was wonderful. When I was trying to explain how I felt she indicated that she understood completely, she having many years of experience. Jennifer explained that the law as it stood gave me complete anonymity. Birthlink would refer to me only as Esther in any correspondence or indeed any other form of contact that they might have with Grace.

When trying to make contact with a birth relative Birthlink initially sends out a letter saying, that a person (Esther in this case) thinks they might be related to them and were they in a certain place at a certain time, in my case Croydon in December 1943. They also stress that neither Birthlink nor the person searching wants to cause any harm or upset. This gives the person being contacted a chance to decide what to do. After one month if there is no reply to the first letter, they then send a second letter. Jennifer explained that perhaps the first letter may have gone astray or that it sometimes takes a second letter to the birth relative for them to make the decision to make contact.

By the end of the interview I was in no doubt that I wanted to go ahead and see if this person in Suffolk was Grace.

Jennifer said that she would go ahead with sending the letter. However, prior to that would I write a letter to Grace telling her a little about my childhood so that it would be available if Grace replied wanting more information. I found that rather difficult, but I managed to put something suitable together.

The other items required by Birthlink were copies of my original birth certificate and the three important pieces of paper that I had found in Mummy's desk. Off we went to Christopher and Janet, to use their printer. That was probably the first time that I really opened up to my family about my feelings regarding my adoption. It got to the point where Janet said, 'Don't tell me anymore, I'm going to cry.'

That evening, Christopher, when searching on the internet, discovered that the Mission of Hope had changed their name and was now called Christian Family Concern. The adoption files that had been with them had been transferred to Croydon social services in 1992 when their adoption agency had closed. Christopher downloaded the history of the Mission of Hope, which made very interesting reading. Thankfully, a person called Janet Ransome Wallis had in 1893 the vision to found a home called The Haven of Hope, which was located in Walthamstow, London E17. This was to be the beginning of several such ventures.

There was a delay in sending the letter to Suffolk, the Royal Mail deciding to go on strike! Finally, the letter went during the second half of November and the waiting started.

I can remember thinking about what I had done with a rising feeling of panic taking over. What was I letting us all in for? I did know that my family were being supportive of me and was aware that I had prayed for God's guidance. Nevertheless, it was quite a step to take.

When at Birthlink, Jennifer had said to me that I should contact Croydon social services to find out if they had a file with my name on it. Jennifer also advised me to contact the adoptions section of Register House in Southport where anyone can register their interest in finding their birth family and vice versa.

I carried on and contacted both Croydon and Southport. Croydon replied by return of post. Yes, they did have a file with my name on it but the assignation of a social worker to the case could take at least three months. In addition, I must have a post adoption counsellor in place for the releasing of my adoption file. This I already had in Jennifer. I was very pleased with the outcome to this letter but did not like the three months wait! This seemed like three years to me. Did they not realise that I was trying to find a mother who was eighty-eight years old and time was an important factor?

The reply from Southport was short and to the point: they were putting me on their contact list but prior to my enquiry nobody had ever tried to find me. I did feel rather sad; however, not everybody knows about such lists.

We, as a family had a brief interlude, a winter break in Aviemore. On our first morning, we awoke to a stunning winter wonderland, everything shimmering as though covered with a multitude of sparkling white diamonds, provided by a thick white frost. It was so incredibly beautiful. Naturally I was continually thinking about the letter, wondering if it had been sent, so was delighted to hear on our return home that it had indeed been posted and was on the way to Suffolk. Now we must wait.

If this was the correct Grace and I was so sure that it was, what would her reaction be? Would she reject me, had she forgotten me? Well, she was receiving this letter about two weeks before my birthday – surely that would jolt her memory?

19

Awaiting Replies

BEING BACK AT HOME did nothing to quell my impatience for a reply to the letter – it was as though I was willing Grace to reply. There was to be no reply to the letter but more importantly, another biblical lesson was about to be learnt.

Exactly one week prior to my birthday, the verse for the day in my Scripture Union notes was as follows – Isaiah chapter 49 verses 15&16: 'Can a mother forget the baby at her breast and have no compassion on the child she has borne? Though she may forget, I will not forget you! See, I have engraved you on the palms of my hands.' I could hardly believe what I was reading. I was in effect being reminded that even if Grace chose to reject me that my loving heavenly Father would never do so and that I was safe and secure, in that knowledge. How thankful I was for this timely reminder.

My emotions were seesawing between being eternally thankful to God and the great desire to find Grace. What I really needed was to remember that God has plans for my life for my good and not to harm me, but I am a human being and often think that I know best.

My birthday came and went like many other birthdays. As a child, I had wonderful birthday parties, which seemed to herald the start of the Christmas party season. School friends plus Aunts from my extended family made up the guest list. The usual party games were the norm including pass the parcel, the grand old Duke of York and pin the tail on the donkey, the donkey being expertly drawn by Daddy. Following this was a delicious birthday tea, lovingly prepared by Mummy and Auntie Lah. Crackers were also the norm for birthday parties but not on Christmas Day. Even now the smell when blowing out candles is so evocative, taking me back all those years to when I was a little girl blowing out the candles on my birthday cake. Perhaps I could create a perfumed candle replicating the mixture of freshly blown out candles and birthday cake icing!

Those birthdays were wonderful for me. However, it is sadly only now that I have considered my parents' feelings. It must have been hard making those birthdays special for me when they were not present at my birth. They had no special memories of that special day in the lives of parents. With hindsight, I realise what special parents they were.

Jennifer had said that if there was no reply to the letter that she would wait until after the New Year before sending the second letter and that is what happened.

Over the Christmas period I found myself singing the carol 'The First Nowell' with renewed vigour. Did Grace, if and when she heard this carol, ever think of Noelle, born so many years before? If she did, I can only imagine how wistful she must have been.

The middle of January arrived and the sending of the second letter to Grace in Suffolk. Now another time of waiting began!

We had a pleasant but brief visit from Maggie (formerly of Essex) who was over from Australia. Maggie naturally wanted to hear the whole story and when I told her that Grace might be living in a village near Saxmundham she very excitedly said 'My sister Jean lives in a village near Saxmundham.' Unfortunately, it turned out not to be the same village.

Sarah had been busy beavering away on the internet and had discovered the emigration of Grace, Eric and their son to Australia, and that Eric had died there, but she also discovered that Grace and her son had returned to this country onboard the *Orantes* arriving at Tilbury on January 28[th,] 1951. Maggie was also very helpful in checking with the Australian records office to see if we could find any further information but that was not to be.

Within two weeks of sending the second letter, I received a telephone call from Jennifer to say that there had been a reply. The reply came from the lady's granddaughter to say that her grandmother was not the lady we were looking for. My heart sank. I said to Jennifer, 'Do you believe her?' 'Yes,' she replied, 'ninety-five per cent, I'll reserve the other five per cent in case we come back to that address.' What an anti-climax! I had been so sure. This time I was certain that God was closing the door to my finding Grace.

However, God moves in mysterious ways and once again, I was given hope that I was indeed doing the right thing by continuing to search. I had decided to read the Bible from Genesis to Revelation in a year and had begun to do this on the 1st January. Addie had given me a special Bible for this purpose as part of his Christmas present to me. I was reading about Moses and amazingly, my daily Scripture Union reading was about Moses too. I was actually reading about a classic case of adoption. Once again, I was having a biblical character brought before me not just once but twice, just as it had been in September/October with the story of Joseph. How remarkable!

Having known the story of Moses from childhood, I had never seen a similarity of his circumstances and my own but they were indeed similar. The mother of Moses loved him so much that she was willing to put her baby in a basket and hide it amongst reeds on the banks of the river Nile. This was to prevent the Egyptians killing baby Moses. His mother must have agonised over what was best for her baby. The story then goes on to tell how Pharaoh's daughter heard the baby crying, had the baby rescued, and eventually went on to adopt the baby Moses.

How Grace must have agonised over what was best for me. Had she loved me so much that she thought it was better to give me up for adoption?

Later in the story of Moses we discover that when a very elderly man he was reunited with his people. I again found myself asking God if this is what He intended to do for me. This was the second time of God showing me how He could allow the removal of someone from his or her birth family, but reunite, him or her many years later. Once more I felt that this was confirmation that I would find Grace.

The search continued. Christopher decided to see if he could find an address for Grace's son. Not knowing his Christian name made it a little difficult! Back to the electoral rolls, he went, this time searching for a person with the same surname as Grace and with a wife called Gillian. It was not too long before he found someone with the Christian names Ronald Eric. This must be him – he had the correct surname and his second name was Eric, the name of Grace's first husband. The electoral roll showed that Ronald had two daughters and their names were there as well. However, after the selling of their house prior to the death of Ronald's wife, Ronald Eric appeared to have vanished. Now we had a problem! We were soon relieved when Christopher found potential addresses for the two daughters.

A telephone call to Jennifer was required. She said that she would only approach the daughters as a last resort, and that she would prefer to go in sideways via one of Grace's siblings of which she had nine. Sarah once more went back to the family tree, but again with the lack of Christian names it made searching difficult. However she did find them, but every lead went cold. Well, we had found out a lot about the family and perhaps that was all I was going to find. Did God not want me to find Grace?

On hearing the latest developments, Jennifer said she would be willing to go in via Grace's son. I wondered how that would be possible as Ronald Eric appeared to have vanished.

The next piece of advice given to me by Jennifer was the hardest thing we had to do. Jennifer suggested that we send for Gillian's death certificate; her husband's name and address would surely be on the certificate if he had done the registration. I recoiled from this as I felt that it was being very intrusive into what I viewed as a very private, personal and sad time for her family. Jennifer assured me that these certificates are public documents and I was entitled to acquire them. We sent for the certificate.

20

Contact is Made

GILLIAN'S DEATH CERTIFICATE duly arrived on the 4th of March 2010. Thankfully, there was an address for Ronald Eric, who we hoped was Grace's son. I contacted Jennifer immediately who said a letter would be sent the following Monday. Another time of waiting began. I was now beginning to be very frustrated. I had lived with Grace's name in my mind for so long and after finding out so much about her, she was no longer just a name but had become a real person. I just wanted to find her.

On Monday the 8th of March, I received a telephone call from Jennifer asking me to come to the office. A letter had arrived from Croydon social services, enclosing a form that I was to sign for the release of my adoption file. I went to Birthlink on Wednesday the 10th of March, saw Jennifer and signed the form from Croydon. Before leaving, I said to Jennifer, 'Did you send that letter on Monday.' 'Yes,' she said, 'but we don't usually get replies by return of post.' I laughed and said, 'No, I expect you'll be sending a second letter in a month's time.'

The following afternoon I was in the garden when Addie shouted to me that Jennifer was on the telephone and wanted to speak to me. I ran into the house, took the receiver from Addie and Jennifer said, 'Hi Esther, I've just been speaking to your niece Debbie.' 'My niece!' I gasped. Jennifer replied, 'Yes, and she had her dad in the room beside her. Debbie also said, "Tell Esther that she is doing no harm, we are glad that she has found us.'" I said, 'What about Grace?' Then Jennifer told me that Debbie had said that unfortunately Granny died some years ago. Debbie then asked what was on my original birth certificate, and Jennifer read out the contents to her. There was no question as to who I was or had been! However, when Jennifer said the name Noelle... there was a gasp at the other end. Jennifer on enquiring if Debbie was all right then had Debbie explain that she was expecting a baby and had said if she ever had a baby girl near to Christmas she would want to name her Noelle. My tears just rolled.

Jennifer then went on to tell me that Debbie and her Dad were going to talk things over that evening and that she would telephone Jennifer again the next day. Jennifer then assured me that everything seemed very positive. I immediately told Addie the good news and could hardly wait for Christopher, Janet, and Sarah to be home from work to relay the news to them.

It slowly began to dawn on me what this news actually meant. Sadly, I had not found Grace. I was so looking forward to meeting her. Well, I should have started this search years earlier while there was still a good chance that she was alive. I would now never know who my father was as only Grace could tell me that. However, I was overjoyed to have made contact with my half-brother and my niece. How thankful I was to God for his guidance to carry on with the search when at times it had seemed in vain. Perhaps God had a good reason why I should not meet Grace and I accept that. What were Ronald and Debbie's thoughts I wondered? This must have been such a shock for them

There was great excitement that evening when giving the news to Christopher, Janet and Sarah – all their hard work had brought about this result. Where would it all lead?

I then told the two close friends who had known about the search and who had been praying for us as the story unfolded. They were both so thankful and elated on hearing the news, telling me that they would continue to pray for the next developments. I of course felt like telling the whole world but I must remain anonymous!

The next day could not come quick enough. What would Debbie say in her next telephone call? Friday dawned, and I waited and I waited and waited. Just as Jennifer was about to leave the office she telephoned me to say that there had been no contact from Debbie. However, Jennifer remained optimistic. I was very down, thinking that Ronald and Debbie had decided that they wanted nothing to do with me. Surely, I had not found them just to lose them again.

It was a long weekend. Monday brought the wonderful sound of the telephone ringing. Lifting the receiver, I heard Jennifer's voice on the other end of the line. She went on to explain that Debbie had had a problem with her car on the Friday and was unable to telephone as planned, for which she sincerely apologised.

The outcome of this telephone call was that Ronald thought I might be his full sister – interesting. He was also quite happy for me to write a letter to him and Jennifer encouraged me to go ahead and write! I said, 'Jennifer, what do I write?' 'Start at the beginning and tell him a little about where you were brought up and the main things in your life. For example, your marriage and family, but do not disclose any names of people or places. When you have completed the letter bring it to the office and it will be posted from here.'

During 2010 I honed my letter writing skills! I started: 'Dear Ronald,' and then I wrote and rewrote and rewrote that letter until I and the family thought it contained enough information to be an introduction to this brother of mine. Finally, I made the journey to Castle Street and delivered the letter to Jennifer for posting. Would I receive a reply? I hoped so – I really hoped that I would.

21

Ronald's Reply

I HAVE ALWAYS thought that I am a reasonably patient person, but not when it came to waiting for a reply from Ronald. The first of April came and there was no reply.

It was Easter and we went off to spend a week with Sarah. On Tuesday the 6th of April, Jennifer telephoned to say that there was a letter from Ronald and my adoption file had arrived. Wow, this was going to be doubly exciting. I arranged to see Jennifer as soon as possible after our return home and on the 9th April, with slight trepidation, I once more climbed the stairs to the Birthlink office.

Sitting beside Jennifer she first handed me Ronald's letter. His very flamboyant handwriting immediately caught my eye. Jennifer commented that she thought he must be very artistic. I opened the letter and started to read. Ronald began by saying that it had been a pleasant surprise to hear from me and continued to say, 'Your parents received one of their best ever Christmas presents, produced by our mother.' So true but it was so lovely of him to put 'our mother.' Following on he said he was 'Giving much, but brief information that would no doubt paint many pictures and draw not a few sketches.' Thereafter followed a list of all the major dates in Grace's life from her birth and including her marriage to his father in November 1939, until her death in 1985.

I looked at Jennifer and said, 'Grace died on Christopher's sixteenth birthday.'

Ronald went on to apologise for the delay in replying to my letter saying he had wished to produce and enlarge some photos for me. He then ended the letter with 'Best Wishes, Ron.' This brief glimpse into the life of Grace was so moving, but there was more to follow. Now we were to look at photos!

I hardly dared look. I was about to see for the first time the face of the mother who had given birth to me over sixty-six years before. I wondered for the last time what she would look like. I was not disappointed. The first photo was of a young Grace taken probably in her late teens/early twenties; so this is what she had probably looked like when I was born. I pointed out to Jennifer how Grace's two upper front teeth crossed ever so slightly just like Sarah's and mine.

First sight of my mother Grace

Another photo was of Grace's mother known as Nan to the family. Now I was seeing my grandmother for the first time. The photo showed an elderly lady with John's baby daughter cradled in her arms and with Ron's eldest daughter standing at her knee. My eye was drawn to the two walking sticks leaning against the fireplace. 'I bet Nan had an arthritic hip,' I said to Jennifer.

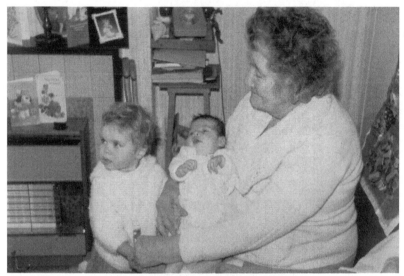

First sight of my grandmother

There was also a photo of Grace with a small Ron beside her somewhere in Australia and when Jennifer looked at the photo, she commented, 'I've seen that look on your face at times.' That one could actually see little similarities between us was so emotive.

I laid aside Ron's letter and photos as Jennifer handed me the adoption file from Croydon, wondering if I was ready for more revelations, as she had previously read it. I was. There could not possibly be very much in it. How wrong I was.

22

Adoption File

I **OPENED THE FILE.** Firstly, a student social worker with the Post Adoption Team in the London Borough of Croydon introduced himself, as the person who had put together a summary of the information contained in the file that related to my adoption. He went on to make me aware that recording standards were not what they are today and that there may be gaps in basic information. I was also to remember the difference in values, attitudes, and the law, between 1943 and the twenty-first century. In addition, I must realise that the people involved with my adoption, including my parents, would not have expected me to have access to the file. Fine, I accepted all that, now please can we go to the next subject on the page, which had the heading: Your Birth.

During the final months of her pregnancy, my birth mother had applied to the Mission of Hope for accommodation at their home for mothers and children in South Croydon, London. A Nursing Sister based at the same RAF base in Essex had referred Grace to the mission.

On the 18th October, 1943, Grace became a resident at the home.While there Grace provided cooking services to the home in order to offset her board and lodgings. How tough that must have been for her. Grace went into the Mayday Hospital Croydon on the 4th December and gave birth to me on the 5th December after a normal delivery. Grace gave me the name Noelle and I weighed 5lbs 14oz.

After my birth, I was breast fed for three weeks before being weaned onto bottle feeds. This piece of information really did affect me. If only I had known that, I would probably have breast fed my children. Part of the reason for my not doing so was my assumption that I had not been breast-fed and therefore there was no need for me to do so when I had my own children.

I started to imagine all the thoughts and feelings that Grace must have had. Not having her baby's father to come and visit her after the birth of her first child. I wondered if anybody had visited her. She also had the very close contact of breast-feeding for three weeks. However, she must have been with me longer than that as she had to wean me onto bottle feeds. Imagine all that time knowing that she was probably going to have to part with me. It must have been heart breaking. These revelations answered my question as to whether I had been on my own that first Christmas. No, I had been with my mother Grace. I am so very glad that we were together that first Christmas and that knowledge is a comfort to me.

The next heading was 'Your Birth Mother.' This indicated Grace's name and age, but there were no recorded descriptions. The file indicated that Grace was in good health, that her religion was Church of England and her home was an address in Romford, possibly that of her mother. Prior to my birth Grace worked as a postal clerk in the WAAF and after leaving the Mission she worked in a factory.

Grace was married to Eric… he had been reported missing presumed dead in the early part of the war.

Grace explained that she had had a relationship with another serving officer also based in the Romford area and had known him for two years prior to my birth. Oh, how glad I was that she really had known him! I wonder, did he know about her being pregnant?

The next heading was 'Your Birth Father.' I could hardly believe my eyes; but there it was in black and white writing. Grace indicated that my natural father's name was Gordon White. 'Gordon White, Gordon White,' I kept repeating it. I had known Grace's name for so long but this was the person who was the other half of me and I thought I would never know who he was. Grace had informed the Mission that Gordon White was a service policeman serving with the Royal Air Force at a base in Essex.

When telling one of my close friends this amazing piece of information she said, 'Oh! That is the "immeasurably more" bit in Ephesians chapter 3 verse 20' – 'Now, to him who is able to do immeasurably more than all we ask or imagine.' I was now experiencing the truth of a verse brought before me many times during my search for Grace.

The next heading was 'Your Adoption.' There is no record of when Grace said goodbye to me but the date of her signing the application form for my admission to the Mission's children's home was the 7th January 1944 and I remained in the care of the nursery staff until an adoptive family was identified. Grace continued to fund my care until my parents took me home to Northumberland, and for sixty-six years, I had been blissfully unaware of most of the trauma surrounding my entrance into this world.

The heading 'Your Adoption' went on to tell of how my adoptive parents were considering adopting a child for a number of months before my birth. Miss Ida Martin, a friend who lived in their area, was responsible for introducing them to the mission. She had told the Mission about their desire to adopt a child and had passed on their details, which led to their application. This was followed up by the usual checks for that era, which were generally a home visit and the taking up of references from friends and professionals who had connections with them.

On the 22nd February 1944, my parents travelled to London, staying there overnight. They arrived at the Mission at 8.30am on the 23rd February. The early morning start was to ensure that they arrived home before dark, for obvious reasons seeing the country was at war. After collecting their precious bundle, they headed to London and on to Northumberland. My mind immediately went back to the tale of the kind gentleman who had offered to carry me up the escalator at King's Cross station. I'm sure he had no idea what a kerfuffle this small baby had caused, but I know Mummy would have thanked him profusely. On the 23rd February, 1944, I unofficially ceased to be Noelle... and became Esther, but it was as though Noelle stayed inside me.

Mummy wrote to the Mission on the 24th February to report that we had arrived home safely about 8pm (so we didn't make it home by dark!) and that I had settled well. At the time of writing Mummy said I was sleeping peacefully in my little cot in the firelight. She then went on to say that my grandfather and Auntie Lah were delighted with me, to say nothing of other family members and friends. This was the first of many annual letters from my parents to update the Mission on my progress, with the letters finally ceasing in 1968.

Mummy with baby Esther

Mummy and Daddy with baby Esther

**Auntie Lah with Daddy with baby Esther
and dogs Rory and Kym**

Following my relocation to the North East the adoption agency arranged visits to see for themselves that all was in order. Visits by a Miss Edith Cork took place on the 18th March and again on the 6th July 1944, the latter date being an unannounced visit. She reported that it was evident that baby Esther was being very well cared for and growing into a charming babe.

This file was continuing to come up with surprises, Edith Cork being the latest. I had known her name all of my childhood and well into adulthood. Edith and my parents always exchanged Christmas cards and I had presumed that she was a missionary, when in fact she was a social worker with the Mission. How extraordinary this whole saga was turning out to be! I am sure Jennifer was wondering what I was going to comment on next!

The Mission was in touch with Grace in the following weeks keeping her up to date with my progress and the adoption process. She had not told her family about her pregnancy and appeared to have little support.

When Grace confirmed that she had no objection to the adoption, my parents applied to the court to have me formally adopted. This was not to be straightforward. Grace at some point heard that Eric was still alive and was a prisoner of war in one of the German 'Stalags'. The court wanted confirmation that Eric was a P.O.W. at the time of my conception to prove that he could not be my biological father. This caused a delay in the court process but was finally resolved with the help and support of Grace. The adoption order was finalised and delivered to Mummy and Daddy on the 12th August 1944. I had officially become Esther Elizabeth…

A whole year had passed since Grace had applied to the Mission for accommodation. The Mission wrote to Grace to tell her that the adoption was official and that was the last correspondence sent to Grace, and there was no further contact received from her.

There was so much to take in. I thought of Grace's feelings, especially when the delay occurred and she had to sort it out. This must have been so distressing for her.

My thoughts turned to Mummy and Daddy. Had they been afraid of losing me? I suspect they had.

23

Letters

THE HEADINGS now changed to 'Extracts from your file.' The extracts were copies of letters sent by Mummy on or near my birthday from 1944 until 1968, telling the Mission about my progress and enclosing a gift for their work. How typical of Mummy. Tellingly there were no letters during my boarding school years. That was proof to me of what it cost Mummy and Daddy not just financially but also emotionally to send me to boarding school. Why? We all suffered so much. What for?

The letters were obviously from a doting mother and some very amusing. At the time of my third birthday, Mummy reported that I had a very strong will and a vivid imagination! (Addie heartily agrees.) I had informed them on my birthday that my new dolly Marie Josie would last me until I took her to heaven with me! I well remember Marie Josie – she was a small jaundiced looking rubber doll. Her limbs and head were removable and I could fully immerse her in water. To be able to dry her thoroughly after her bath, I literally took her apart! Marie Josie went to dolly heaven a long time ago, but I still have her clothes, lovingly made by Auntie Lah.

In 1961 Mummy wrote of remembering the wintry day in 1944 on which they had travelled to collect me, also the long journey home. It must have been quite a journey. I don't think Mummy would ever have given a baby their bottle or even changed a nappy and Daddy, well I don't think so!

The last letter sent in December 1968 by Mummy said:

'Our dear Esther is now 25 years old and we are so looking forward to the birth of her baby next April. It is a great joy to us and I am sure you too will rejoice with us. She and her husband are very happy and going on with the Lord. All being well we shall spend Christmas and New Year with them in Edinburgh. We miss her so much but feel so thankful for her happiness.'

Following on from this were a copy of the application form for my admission to the Mission of Hope dated the 7th January 1944, and my medical report, both of which were straightforward.

I had been amazed at the letters sent to the Mission by Mummy, but nothing could have prepared me for the three letters that were to follow. These letters were the original, handwritten letters from Grace, sent to the Mission during the first few weeks after my parents had taken me to my new home in Seahouses.

The first letter on the 8th March 1944 sent by Grace was enclosing money for my keep; also, she tells of having to work in a factory from 8am to 7.30pm and of being on night shift. Towards the end of the letter, she says: 'I'm so glad that baby Noelle went off to be with grand people, I pray she will settle down well with her parents and I know God will bless her and keep her in his keeping.'

How very prophetic! My mind flashed back to me standing in the idyllic cemetery of Spittalford, situated between

Embleton and Craster in north Northumberland, this being where the grave of my paternal grandparents is. I had many times stood by their grave, but on the last occasion I had been particularly struck by the very similar words which are engraved on their headstone – 'In God's Keeping' – and now I was reading them almost as a blessing to me from Grace.

The second letter on the 9th April 1944 which must have been Easter Sunday, as Grace after asking if a representative from the Mission had visited dear little Noelle, went on to say that she had been to a grand Easter service that morning and that she loved going to Chapel.

Next, she wrote:

'I also feel as though I love you all at "Bird Hirst", for that is where I found the true meaning of love and kindness and also a Great Friend, and I thank you all for all your kindness and for all I learnt there, which has meant so much to me and always will. God Bless and cheerio, trusting you found Noelle well and contented.'

Oh, how thankful I felt knowing that she had had such a happy experience at the Mission and she mentions finding a Great Friend – I wonder if she found Jesus; certainly I am sure that she had heard about Him. One of my regrets already put right before I was born.

The mood changed with the third letter, written just one week later. On the16th April 1944, Grace was obviously very distressed when she wrote:

'Please pardon me for writing to you this way, but may I have my baby back? I just recently told my sister and she has offered me a home for my baby and insists on me getting her back. I was so worried about her and kept wishing and wanting to get her, as I love children, and as she is mine, I love her more so. I feel that nothing else matters, there is a way to keep her and I do so want her. Please forgive me, but please will you get her back for me, I really and truly need her. Will you kindly let me know what you can do as soon as possible. I will pay any expenses if wanted. Yours Truly, Mrs G...'

'Oh! How awful! Why didn't they do something?' Jennifer turned to me and quietly said, 'Turn the page.' I turned the page. A copy of a telegram ended the nightmare.

The telegram sent from Romford at eight minutes past two and received in Croydon at fourteen minutes past two on the 17th April 1944, the day after the sending of the third letter was as follows: Miss Smith, 14 South Park Road, South Croydon. 'Kindly ignore letter regarding baby. Grace...'

'Why did she change her mind?' I asked. Jennifer replied, 'Maybe someone else in the family found out and told her to leave well alone.' Well I could now never doubt how much she wanted to keep me and how absolutely unbearable it must have been for her to give me up for adoption.

Jennifer and I went over the contents of the file once more. There was so much to take in. I was quite overwhelmed. I went home to ponder.

Ponder I did! All the way home on the bus. So much information to take in and what surprises! On reaching home, I related everything to Addie and he read Ron's letter and the adoption file for himself. When seeing the photograph of Grace his comment was, 'She was a good looking woman!'

Once again, I could hardly wait for Christopher, Janet and Sarah to be home from work so that I could tell them all that I had discovered in the course of one afternoon. It was truly amazing.

Before leaving Birthlink, Jennifer suggested that I write another letter to Ron. This letter was to have some photographs enclosed which should be clear and perhaps enlarged so that features could be clearly seen. Jennifer said, 'Ron and family will pore over them just like you are doing.' I duly came up with a selection of photographs and less than a week later I found myself writing once more to Ron.

In this letter, I was able to give him more information, but nothing that would reveal my identity, such as Addie having been an accountant but not the company where he had worked. I couldn't say what Christopher did. When googling someone in his profession, working in Scotland, with the name Christopher he would have been very easily identified. This was also true of Sarah, very clandestine.

I did so look forward to Ron's next letter, which I hoped would come quite soon.

24

My Sister's Voice

APRIL BECAME MAY, May became June and there was no reply from Ron. Had he decided that he did not want to know this sister so recently found? Jennifer however remained upbeat but did decide to contact Debbie to see if all was well.

Addie and I went to Yorkshire during the last week in June to attend the funeral of a friend, leaving Sarah at home in Edinburgh as she was spending a few days holiday with us. After the funeral on Friday 25th June 2010 when travelling back home my mobile phone rang. It was Sarah. 'Hello Mum, Jennifer has left a message, she has had a telephone call from Ron and he sent a message for you.' 'Really, what was it?' 'It was "May the road rise to meet you, May the wind always be at your back, May the sun shine warm upon your face."' To me it sounded like some sought of blessing. How intriguing. It is indeed an Irish blessing written by an anonymous writer and continues: 'May the rains fall softly upon your fields, and until we meet again, May God hold you in the palm of His hand.' Another blessing, this time from my brother!

I telephoned Jennifer first thing on the Monday morning and she said that she had had a lengthy conversation with Ron who apparently had been in contact with Birthlink not long after my letter to him. Jennifer had been on holiday. Thankfully, all was well and we could resume contact. Ron told Jennifer that he was not good at letter writing and wondered if I would like our sister Sandra to write to me as he felt that she had spent much longer with Grace and could probably answer more of my questions. Of course, I was delighted at the prospect of having contact with Sandra, so Jennifer emailed her to say that I would welcome a letter from her.

I hadn't long to wait as Sandra wrote to me on the 28thJune. A few days later, I went to Birthlink to receive the first letter from my sister. It was lovely to receive a letter from Sandra telling me about herself and also telling me that when she was about 13/14 years of age Grace had told her that she could have had a much older sister but that she had unfortunately been 'lost'. Grace had said this with regret and of course, Sandra had interpreted this information in a completely different way to what had actually happened. To me this answered my question as to whether Grace had forgotten about me. Now I knew she had not forgotten. Thirty-three years or more after my birth, she had still been remembering me.

This revelation and those original letters from Grace about me to the Mission had given me a close awareness of Grace and her love for me, especially the letters. It is as if she were talking to me. This person was so very much more than a name to me now. When I thought and indeed think about her, I could and can see a face and that is something that I cherish. I wish I could have a mental picture of Gordon White!

Sandra next wrote in the middle of July with more information about nieces and nephews, cousins and Grace's siblings. A non-essential fact, but an amusing one was, according to Sandra, she had never had white stilettos in her wardrobe; well, I may not have been an Essex girl but I had the white stilettos!

Ron's second letter arrived which was a very long interesting epistle – so much for him not being good at letter writing! It was in this letter that Ron informed me that our grandfather had been a bigamist. Up until then I had coped with everything, but this triggered a real wave of emotion and it was the first time that I felt like walking away. I cried myself to sleep that night, but I knew that I could not walk away from Ron or Sandra. God had been gracious enough to let me find them and I knew that I wanted to be in touch with my birth family and needed to know this sort of information as it is part of my background.

I think my being upset was perhaps something that was waiting to happen. I do not readily show my feelings; they are generally kept firmly under control. This was probably the trigger point that led to the release of much pent up emotion and was most likely a good thing. Tears rolling down one's cheeks are extremely therapeutic compared to the silent ones inside. Anybody discovering information about his or her birth family needs to be aware that any revelation can act as a trigger to unforeseen emotion.

Sometime later Sandra asked me what Christopher and Sarah thought about their disreputable family and I said, 'Oh they don't think you're disreputable, Sandra,' to which she replied, 'I didn't mean me, I meant our grandfather.' I answered that it does not matter what our grandfather did or was, but what we ourselves have become. It was a sobering moment.

Christopher kept urging me to have telephone contact as he wanted to move things on so that we could arrange a meeting. Sandra had already said that she would be willing for us to meet sometime in the future. Jennifer was quite happy for me to have telephone contact but on my mobile, so that there was no likelihood of anybody tracing me through an Edinburgh number. I was to arrange a suitable time for the call to take place. However, I felt that I knew enough about my 'down south family' for them to have my home number, so I decided to wait until I could reveal my identity.

Towards the end of August, Christopher announced that he had my birthday weekend off and thought it would be an ideal time to meet with some of my new family. Once more, I turned to Jennifer and asked if I could not have telephone contact and reveal my identity, as we would like to try to arrange a meeting at the beginning of December. The answer was yes! Jennifer advised me to write to Ron and Sandra simultaneously giving them my address and telephone number, saying that I was ready for contact by telephone. This I did immediately and took the letters to Jennifer on Thursday August 26th, 2010, for her to send with a covering letter.

The following morning Addie and I had been out. As Addie put his key into the door the telephone started to ring. He opened the door, picked up the receiver and I heard him say, 'Yes, she's here.' He handed me the receiver, saying, 'I don't know who it is.' I said, 'Hello.' The voice at the other end replied: 'Hi, it's Sandra.' I didn't recognise the voice, so I said 'Sandra?' 'Yes, it's your sister Sandra,' she replied.

My sister Sandra! I was nearly speechless; the letter had only been posted the day before, and it was now barely midmorning. Sandra explained that she had the day off work as she was waiting for the gasman. The letter had arrived. She had telephoned Jennifer and then immediately telephoned me. The telephone call lasted for one hour and ten minutes! I can't remember what we talked about but it was non- stop. Addie kindly brought me coffee! At the end of the call I said something about having a sister to which Sandra replied, 'But you've two, Sue wants to know about you too.' I had actually spoken to my sister Sandra and that was quite incredible.

Sandra wrote to me the following day enclosing photos and saying it was lovely to talk and was hoping that I would want to continue, as she certainly did.

One week later, I dialled Sandra's telephone number to thank her for the photos she had sent. It was a good excuse for me to make that first call to her. Sandra answered and said that she was in the process of writing to me and was wrapping up a package for me. She then asked, 'Do you know what tatting is?' 'Yes, it's similar to crocheting,' I replied. Sandra was wrapping up a pair of Grace's gloves, made for Grace when she was young by a relative of hers. Would I like to have the gloves, she wondered, and then hand them down to Sarah? I said I would love to have them! Sandra was very emotional that evening as she had been looking at photos that I had sent to her and she said, 'One of the photos that you sent me of you when you were very small is very like one of myself when very small.'

The package duly arrived with the gloves beautifully wrapped in a small bag. I tried them on and they fitted. Not only did I have a name, a picture, her handwritten letters, but now something that had actually belonged to Grace. Sandra had given me something that she treasured. I will do likewise as I am sure Sarah will too. This touching act of generosity told me much about my newly discovered sister. I loved her for it.

25

Emotional Meeting

DURING OUR ANNUAL HOLIDAY at Bassenfell Christopher contacted me to say that *The Scotsman* newspaper had a special offer for cheap rail tickets to London. Christopher had collected the required tokens and thought that if we intended to meet with family over my birthday weekend we should not delay in booking. I plucked up courage and telephoned Sandra to see what she thought of the idea. Her answer was that we should go ahead with booking the tickets.

I contacted Avios (air miles) and successfully booked a hotel for the five of us to stay during the first weekend in December. That year my birthday was on the Sunday. Sandra said that she would come to London on the Saturday and maybe John, my other half-brother, might come for lunch. Sandra would stay overnight. Ron would come on Sunday and we would have a birthday lunch together. One year on from the sending of the first letter to the address in Suffolk, I had found the right family and was now going to be able to meet some of them. What an amazing year it had turned out to be.

During the second part of October I received my next letter from Ron. Having told him that I did a lot of cycling when a teenager and having described the beautiful Northumbrian coast and countryside, he made this comment: 'Cycling with your friend through sunlit dappled country lanes, where butterflies like marionettes dance on hedgerows, scented breeze and blackbirds hang high, as blue and fluffy clouds scurry by.' I realised then that I had a rather poetic brother and future writings have captivated me. 'Thank you Ron.' A suggestion of his was that I might like to start and write a novel about a lost family. No Ron, I could never do that, I told him when answering his letter.

The letter ended with him saying that he had heard about and was looking forward to our meeting in December. Ron also said, 'Thanks for your telephone number at the end of which a Scottish lilt resides! I'll call after this letter drops on your mat.' Oh dear, I hoped he wouldn't be disappointed with my accent!

True to his word, he duly called me one Saturday. He said, 'Hello, I'm Ron, I think I'm your brother.' 'Yes, I think you are,' I said. This was to be an even longer call than the first chat with Sandra, the call lasting over two hours! We talked about anything and everything.

Towards the end of November 2010 we stayed with friends who were holidaying in the Aviemore area and found ourselves coming home in a blizzard. It was to be the beginning of a very bad winter. This put in jeopardy our meeting with the family. The news was not good, roads were bad, trains cancelled or delayed and airports closed. We were going to have to make a decision. I telephoned Sandra to find out how she felt; she then told me how icy their roads were. They were willing to travel, were we?

Addie and I did a trial walk up the hill to the top of the road with our luggage; it was a struggle – no taxi would venture down the road and the bus service to the station was questionable. By the Thursday it became apparent that it was futile to carry on with our plans. I did not want anybody to take the risk, however disappointing it was for me. There would be another time.

I telephoned Avios. Our insurance would cover the miles I had used for the hotel, but strictly speaking, we might have been able to travel. However, Avios and the hotel were extremely sympathetic and said that they were willing for us to rebook if we did so straight away. After some frantic telephone calls to the family, I was able to book for the second weekend in March. Our train fares were non-refundable. Christopher and Janet had decided to fly, so their airfares were lost but it was a small price to pay for everyone's safety.

On the Saturday, a lovely basket of roses arrived from Sandra to help make up for our disappointment. On my birthday we were well and truly snowed in. Happily, Christopher and Janet managed to get to us bringing a most attractive looking and equally delicious birthday trifle made by Janet.

I may not have met them on my birthday but both Sandra and Ron telephoned me to say happy birthday. Sandra at one point had said, 'Oh you'll get your first birthday card with to my Sister on it'—and true to her word I received one, only a little late. A novel experience.

Sue, my other half sister, was over from New Zealand spending Christmas with her family. Sandra, John, Sue and Ron had been having a meal together at Sandra's home and she had taken the opportunity to video them during which they sent their Christmas greetings to me.

On Christmas Day Sandra telephoned to say Happy Christmas and each one of the family was able to have his or her first words with a newly found Aunt. A Very Happy Christmas.

Eventually March 11th arrived, exactly one year since Debbie made the first contact telephone call. Addie, Christopher, Janet and I boarded the train at Edinburgh Waverly, destination London King's Cross. Sarah joined the train at York and we were off on a family adventure. We arrived safely, checked into our hotel and then made our way to meet Sandra. Jennifer had advised us to meet in a public place for our first get-together and we had agreed on the National

Gallery. As we approached the gallery we could see Sandra waiting outside – she saw us as we waited to cross the road. Poor Sandra, she was all on her own about to meet five newly discovered relatives. Neither Ron nor John could come, Ron being in New Zealand visiting Sue. That first hug from my sister was just wonderful.

We went inside the gallery and Christopher, Janet and Sarah went off to explore. This we had prearranged so that I could have a little time on my own with Sandra. Addie went off and brought back a cup of tea for us to enjoy together. I can't remember what we talked about. I was just so pleased to be in the company of my sister. Later we all went out for a meal. I hadn't much sleep that night but had the prospect of seeing Sandra the following morning.

We had chosen the British Museum for our second meeting where we posed for photos outside. Once inside Sandra and I settled ourselves at a table with a cup of coffee while the rest of the family went off in different directions. I had my adoption file with me so I was able to let Sandra read it for herself. When she read the letters written by Grace, she said, 'Mum's writing didn't change.' Then there were tears, those letters being so very poignant.

Sandra needed to catch an afternoon train back to her home in Essex so after another coffee with the family we said our very emotional goodbyes. Sandra was planning to go to New Zealand for an unlimited time and she was very keen to visit us in Edinburgh before leaving in July, and I was so delighted that she wanted to come. We then left each other knowing that another meeting was not too far away.

26

Visiting Edinburgh

THE NEXT FEW WEEKS were a hive of activity in
Edinburgh. Earlier on in 2011, we had booked the painter
for the month of May to do a few small jobs in the house and
then the outside, including the snowceming of the walls. Ron
had returned from New Zealand and when hearing that Sandra
was coming to Edinburgh had asked if he could join her. We of
course were delighted that he should want to come and I said
'Yes.' Sarah was coming for the weekend too, to meet her new
uncle. This meant that all bedrooms were required. I now
needed to return what was once Christopher's bedroom and has
now become my ironing, creating and computer room back into
a bedroom. It needed some serious work in emptying and
tidying but eventually I deemed it presentable.

The weather was not kind during May and the painter was
very behind with his work. Thankfully, during the last days of
the month, the weather improved and he was able to finish after
I had left for the station to meet Ron and Sandra! I had ended
up explaining to the painter why I needed him to be finished.
He was fascinated by my story and on a future visit two years
later he asked how my new family were doing.

Friday 3rd June was as perfect a summer's day that you will
ever get in Edinburgh, warm and sunny. Christopher drove me
to the station to meet Ron and Sandra. Yes, I recognised Ron
from his photograph and it was lovely to be able to welcome
both of them to Edinburgh. Sandra had visited to attend a
wedding in the nineteen eighties but this was Ron's first visit,

although he told me that he had once been to Inverness. On arriving home, Addie and Christopher joked that we didn't have the house newly painted for every visitor.

Much conversation followed with Janet joining us after work, but we did eventually sit down to a meal. Ron being a vegetarian, we introduced him to vegetarian haggis, and he pronounced it good. Sarah arrived home later that evening to join in all the chat. Wondering what to do the next day, we decided it would be good for all of us to go out together the following morning and that a city bus tour would be a good way for Ron and Sandra to have a snapshot tour of our beautiful city.

Alas, we awoke the next morning to a complete change in the weather. Where was all the sunshine? The city was now enveloped in the notorious east coast haar, a cold sea mist that seeps right through your very being, a truly horrible day. We decided to brave the weather and set off to catch a bus into the city. We were to meet Christopher and Janet at the Waverley Bridge bus stop. Arriving before them, Sarah decided to buy an extra layer of clothing to keep out the cold, she having come dressed for summer. Janet followed shortly after on the same quest. Apart from the weather, the tour was very enjoyable. On completing the tour, we were so cold that we immediately sort refuge in Jenners department store to be heated up by some hot coffee.

After our warm interlude we set off again, only six of us this time, as Addie very wisely decided to go home. The rest of us walked to the Castle to look at the views from the esplanade. How disappointing that they hardly existed. Retreating down the Royal Mile we called in at the Hub to have a welcome lunch break.

Where next? We agreed on a walk down The Royal Mile but only four brave souls set off – Ron, Sandra, Sarah and I. I hasten to add that Christopher and Janet went home to pack as they were going on holiday the next day and we were all going out to have a meal together in the evening. The four of us set off and walked to the Palace of Holyrood House, having a brief visit to St Giles Cathedral on the way down where Ron enjoyed having his photo taken beside the statue of John Knox. We viewed the palace through the railings and then decided to call it a day.

The bus that we caught to go home happened to be on a route that went past the old Royal Infirmary. Not to be deterred, we alighted and walked in the grounds to view where I had done my nurses training. I recounted many tales such as Addie throwing snowballs at Angela's bedroom window so that she could get me to speak to him. We completed the day by having a lovely evening meal at a small village on the East Lothian coast.

We spent Sunday morning looking at the adoption file. Ron had not seen this before and there were yet more tears. The photograph albums came out with Sarah producing school photographs of both her and Christopher. As Sandra went through the albums every so often she would exclaim, 'You look like Mum there.' She also kept seeing resemblances between Sarah and other members of the family; this was all very interesting. Sarah left at teatime and Ron, Sandra and I went for a lovely walk in the locality.

This had been an extremely memorable and enjoyable weekend, which ended all too soon. Our parting at the station was hard. Sandra and I did not know when we might see each other again but we knew that we did want to and promised to keep in touch on a regular basis, as did Ron and I.

The day after Ron and Sandra left, a lovely bouquet of flowers arrived to say thank you for having them to stay, which was so kind of them. That was not all. The next day another delivery was made, a large box containing a beautiful rose bush with masses of very pale pink blooms, the name of the rose being 'Special Child.' I telephoned Ron straight away as Sandra was at work and I said, 'Ron, I have received another delivery today from you and Sandra.' 'Yes I know, Sandra said she was going to have it sent.' 'Do you know what the rose is called?' 'I can't remember but I know Sandra chose it because of the name.' I spoke to Sandra later that day and she said, 'Well, you were a special child.' I really didn't know what to say, except thank you. A fortnight later over the telephone Sandra gave me the reasons of why I was a special child in a little verse called 'Special Child' that she had composed:

The special child was conceived in love by Grace.
The special child was born in love by Grace.
The special Child was given in love by Grace.
The special child was nutured in love by my parents.
The special child has grown in love with Addie.
The special child has been kept in love by the
Grace of God.

Sandra gave this to me on the 18th June 2011. The third line, added by Sarah, the sixth line added by me, both approved by Sandra. What a remarkable, sequence of events.

Sandra left for New Zealand a few weeks later.

Communication with both Ron and Sandra continued by telephone, letter, email and Skype which was to be the means of my first direct contact with my other sister Sue; not only could I speak to her but I was able to see her as well in New Zealand. I must now bow to the wonders of modern technology!

After Sandra had been in New Zealand for several months, she decided that she would like to stay on. She had a return ticket so was going to take the opportunity to return to the UK for a visit and asked if she could come and see us. Of course, I replied that she could.

Her visit was to be in the middle of April 2012 and Ron was to accompany her. I really did hope that the weather would be kind. I had previously asked them if they would like to visit Northumberland to see where I spent my childhood and they replied that they would. We decided to follow the advice of the weather forecast and proceeded to go there on the first day of their visit.

Travelling along the scenic A1 coast road our first stop was at The Barn at Beal, a lovely spot just before the causeway over to Holy Island (Lindisfarne if you are not local). Ron, Sandra, Addie and I along with Christopher and Janet sat drinking coffee while enjoying the wonderful coastal scenery. On arriving in Seahouses, we met up with Sarah at the Bamburgh Castle Hotel where I had reserved a table overlooking the harbour.

After lunch and a walk on the pier, we made our way up the main street pointing out the Chapel where we as a family had worshipped and where Addie and I had been married. We passed the shops and the houses where various friends and family had lived. Then we reached the primary school where I had gone to school. A little way up the road but on the opposite side, we came to 'Romany,' my childhood home with all the happy and sad memories. Retracing our steps, we passed the school and turned into an opening leading to the old railway line where we went to see the recently replaced seat in memory of Daddy. We stood looking over the school playing field to 'Romany' just as he had done so many times when out walking the dogs.

I wondered what Mummy and Daddy would have thought about me standing there with my brother and sister. If they had lived to know me as I am now, they would have been very sure of how I would cherish all my memories of them, and how I would not have wanted any other parents. However, at this stage in my life, it was good and right for me to know the family from which I had originated.

Our time in Northumberland ended with us having a cup of tea in neighbouring Bamburgh, another special village that I have spent so much time in during different periods of my life.

We then headed for home via the inland route, firstly towards the Cheviots, then into Scotland crossing the River Tweed at Coldstream. I eventually pointed out the Eildon hills, explaining that my boarding school had been in that direction. Later when we reached the top of Soutra, we took in the wonderful panorama stretching out to Edinburgh and over the Firth of Forth. Finally, on towards the artificial ski slope on the Pentland Hills with home not far away.

Next day the weather, which had been reasonable the day before, once more proved disappointing. However, we did go out for coffee and lunch, at one point taking Ron and Sandra to see the Forth Rail and Road Bridges. Ron being absolutely captivated with the railway bridge, said, 'Oh, please can we just sit and look at it.'

Later that afternoon we went to see Jennifer so that she could meet Ron and Sandra. All concerned really enjoyed the time we spent talking together. After seeing Jennifer, we walked along Princes Street to Ron's favourite store, Jenners, where we had yet another cup of tea. The day ended with us having our evening meal with Christopher and Janet at their home. Ron and Sandra left the following morning and this time I really did have no idea when I might see Sandra again.

Ron came back to visit at the beginning of June 2013 which was most enjoyable, especially as we had a wonderful summer's day in which to visit Edinburgh Castle, stopping every so often for refreshments as it was exceedingly warm. The views over the city and the Firth of Forth were excellent even with a slight heat haze and Ron really did enjoy himself. Ron went to church with us on the Sunday morning and I think he found it all very interesting. After lunch, Janet and I took Ron for a walk in the Pentland Hills beside Threipmuir reservoir, which proved to be very popular.

The following day we were able to take Ron to the home of golf at St Andrews and as we crossed the road bridge over the Firth of Forth Ron was delighted to see the railway bridge again.

At one point Ron and I enjoyed a chat while sitting having a cup of tea in the garden. He was telling me more about Grace when I said to him, 'Well, I suppose I must have something of her in me.' He replied with tears in his eyes, 'I see it more and more.'

All too soon it was time for Ron to head back home. We parted, saying that we as a family would explore the possibility of having a holiday in Essex during 2014, when we hoped to meet my brother John and his wife, as well as Debbie and any other family members that would like to meet us. Ron was very eager to show me where Grace had lived with her parents at the address we had come back to so many times when searching for the family.

27

Family Memories

BY TALKING with Grace's family (my half-brothers and sisters and my niece Debbie), I have had a glimpse into Grace's life which has given me a snapshot of my birth mother. Grace was someone who endured much grief and distress, through many circumstances out-with her control and had very difficult decisions to make. The snapshot, however, also portrays someone with a great love for her family and for others with whom she had contact. How I would have loved to meet her. I admire her ability and strength to be able to carry on when at times life must have seemed intolerable.

Grace was the second child of her parents and grew up living in the family home in Romford. I have little information about her childhood, but know that she was not overly fond of her father who was a strong disciplinarian and used to hit Grace with the buckle end of his belt! No wonder she couldn't reveal her pregnancy to those at home.

Before her marriage to Eric, Grace worked at a tearoom in Romford where her baking skills were put to good use, she being an excellent baker, and I'm sure The Mission benefited greatly when she cooked there. Very romantically, the name of the tearoom was 'The Tryst' and romance was indeed in the air. Eric was a police officer stationed at the Police Station in Romford, which was practically next door to 'The Tryst'! Sue has told me that the tree where they did their courting is still in a nearby roundabout after several people including Grace campaigned to have it kept.

Eric joined the army at the beginning of the war and he and Grace were married in November of that year, but very sadly, Grace received a telegram probably during 1940 saying that Eric was missing, presumed dead. The presumption then would have been that Grace was a widow. We of course now know that Eric was in fact captured by the Germans in May 1940.

Just over a year later, in 1941, Grace joined the WAAF and was eventually stationed at RAF Hornchurh in Essex. This was where she was to be for the vast majority of her time in the WAAF. Nobody seems to know where Grace lived after her discharge from the WAAF and before her admittance to The Mission, but we do know that she went home to Romford after she left The Mission. Not being sure at what point Grace learnt that Eric was in a POW camp, one could presume that it was after she became pregnant with me and this would have made her situation even more complex.

Eric's release would have no doubt triggered many emotions for both of them but thankfully, they were able to continue their life together and were also to have the pleasure of going on to have Ron and also starting a new life in Australia. Tragically, this situation was to last only five years. Eric was a POW in StalagXXA and all of the survivors suffered from liver damage, the result of experiments that took place in the camp. Realising that death was not far away, he wanted to return to England to die. The ship was still very close to Sydney when Eric became critically ill and died. It was Armistice Day and Sue has told me that Grace couldn't bear to hear the Last Post. Ron attributed his father's death to what he termed Germanic philosophy.

The burial of Eric took place in a cemetery north of Sydney where many years later Ron was able to visit his father's grave. Grace must have wondered what would happen to them. She had very little money, a small son of not quite five years old and no home. Fortunately, a younger sister of Grace was also in Australia and came to the rescue with Grace and Ron staying in her sister's sleep out (a shed), where they remained until Grace had enough money for the fare home to England. We know from Sarah's discovery of their names on the passenger list of the *Orantes* that they arrived back in this country at the end of January 1951. One of Grace's brothers and his wife met them at Tilbury and Ron told me that it was his first memory of life.

On arriving back in England, Grace and Ron went to live in Romford with Grace's mother and times were very tough, her mother having small children of her own, Grace's half siblings. Ron told me that his Mum had gone away for a while which is when she gave birth to a baby boy named Ian who was also adopted. Her son Ian was to find Grace many years later and she and the family continued to keep in touch with him until his death.

In the autumn of 1953 Grace married Richard. The family have told me how they idolised each other and were an extremely happy family with their son, two daughters and Ron. 'My stepfather Richard was calm, thoughtful and sensible but above all a nice person,' was Ron's description of him. There have been many happy and amusing tales told of this period of Grace's life. She continued to be an excellent baker and cook and Ron wrote in a letter to me that Grace never liked walking past cream cakes – they were a form of art and worthy of occasional discussions! In the same letter he described how he could still hear the sound of clashing, knitting needles. He also conjured up a wonderful picture of him sitting opposite Grace, with the palms of his hands approximately two feet apart, thumbs raised, and eight fingers pointing towards her that were holding a skein of wool, which was being converted into a ball of wool ready for use.

Grace had a great love of gardening and apparently kept a pair of scissors in her bag just in case she needed to take a cutting! All these shared memories and descriptions have shown me that Grace was indeed a true home-maker. However, after fourteen happy years tragedy was to strike again with the death of Richard in February 1968. Grace was devastated. Only forty-six and widowed twice. Now Grace had three young children to bring up on her own and Ron also at home.

Approximately seven years later Grace was to remarry. Ron wrote that this new husband was not appreciated by those who came to know him and after a short time, Grace was apparently persuaded by family members to seek a divorce. This was a situation that she found extremely difficult.

Grace was very involved with charity groups associated with the RAF and was instrumental in the placing of a memorial at the site of the Hornchurch Aerodrome. November would find Grace selling poppies, one year collecting the most money. That was interesting to hear as I sold poppies for a number of years. Grace would also be a standard- bearer at services and parades on Remembrance Day. Having done so much to help the 'Guinea Pig Club', they bestowed an honorary membership on Grace.

Through her tireless work for RAFA, Battle of Britain and Hornchurch charity groups, Grace met 'Blackie', a widower, who she married. They had a wonderful, extremely happy time together, which was very sadly cut short by the very sudden death of Grace while on holiday in France. This must have been a tremendous shock for all the family and Ron told me that he was in his study when he received the telephone call, telling him that his Mum had died and how he just could not believe it. At her funeral, Grace was given a guard of honour, quite rare for a civilian and it showed how highly she was thought of.

The end of a remarkable life, which all these years later is still being remembered with love, affection and gratitude by all her family.

28

Essex without Ron

DURING THE AUTUMN of 2013 we started to look for a holiday property within easy reach of Ron's home. Christopher was quite adamant that it should be large enough so that Ron could stay overnight if he wished which we all thought was a very good idea. We chose a converted barn with plenty of room, about three quarters of an hour's drive from Ron's home. The barn was booked and we all looked forward to the first week in May 2014 when we were due to be on holiday.

The New Year text message to me from Ron was 'Appy n year esther…addie…chris… janet an sarah an 2b completed book of yr life.'

Ron was always enquiring as to how the book was developing, he being one of the first people to suggest that I might put my story into a book. Now he was asking if it would be finished in time for May. I told him that I rather doubted that but we would see. I was hoping for a suitable ending to this epistle and had hopes of finding it in Essex!

When I was at one stage unsure as to how I could best describe my feelings, I received an inspirational e-mail from Ron so I confess that there are several phrases used in this book that are thanks to Ron.

One further text message received from Ron towards the end of January indicated that he hoped that my guided, thoughtful, ink-driven pen was spilling lots of ink, and that he realised that it was not easy to paperise one's thoughts.

Towards the end of February I had a longish chat with Sue on Skype, which was good. Feeling that I had come to know Sue a little better over the previous months and realising it would be her birthday very soon I decided to make her a birthday card and email it to her. Sue very promptly sent me a thank you email. I thought how lovely it was to have a sister and of course, I have two!

Two days later the telephone rang. I answered and a voice said, 'Esther, this is Debbie, Ron's daughter.' I knew instinctively that there must be something wrong. I had never spoken to Debbie before and it was early in the morning so her telephoning me could only mean bad news. It was very, very bad news. Debbie continued to tell me of how Ron was in hospital on a life support machine, having sustained serious life threatening injuries following an attack on him at his home.

I have experienced death of close family and friends in the past but this was something that one only reads about in newspapers or hears on the news and now it had happened to somebody that I was close to. I could not comprehend it and I certainly remained in a dreamlike state for the rest of the day. How could this have happened to Ron who seemed to be a very gentle person?

I will refrain from giving any more details of this horrific time only to say that very sadly Ron died less than a week after his admission to hospital.

Now I would have no more diverse and interesting telephone calls from Ron, no more quirky text messages to inspire me, and no more envelopes addressed in his unique handwriting dropping through the letterbox. Why?

I realised that some people knowing of my Christian faith would ask the question as to why God allowed this to happen and I would have to answer that I do not know the reason. Why did He allow Ron to die and disappear from my life when I had so recently found him? I have no answer, but I know that God has a plan for my life, a plan, which I do not know about and which may be very different to the way I would plan it. However, I know that continuing to put my trust in Him, in whatever circumstances I find myself, is the best way. He will come into all aspects of my life and meet me just where I am at any given moment. Jesus understands our human situations very well, he having experienced them when he was here on earth. It actually tells us in the Gospel of St. John chapter 11 verse 35 that 'Jesus wept' when his friend Lazarus died so he knows the pain felt at times like these.

We were going to Keswick for our usual March week. I did not feel like going but we did go and I felt a little better as the week went on. The day before we went, Debbie telephoned and we had a long conversation during which she asked if I would like to attend Ron's funeral. I had very mixed feelings about it. On one hand, I would most certainly have liked to attend but on the other hand, I did not want to intrude on a very sad and emotional occasion. Neither Sue nor Sandra were going to be able to go, as they had flown over from New Zealand while Ron was in hospital, and were now back home. I would be meeting more of the family for the first time and that would incur added emotion, which I was reluctant to do, especially having had no direct contact with my other brother John. I told Debbie that I would think it through and asked her to keep me informed. The funeral would not be taking place for several weeks owing to the circumstances of Ron's death so I had time to consider what I should do.

Addie asked me what I wanted to do about our proposed holiday in Essex at the beginning of May. All the plans and emotions of the visit would be so different now. Debbie had said she wanted to meet us and would like to show us where Ron lived, which I really appreciated. How thoughtful of her in the midst of her own loss and grief.

159

Should we cancel the holiday? No. We had arranged this holiday for all our family. Christopher, Janet and Sarah had taken annual leave so that we could all be together and we must still go. We would look forward to meeting Debbie and just maybe my brother John.

Time passed and I was no clearer in my mind as to what the answer would be concerning my going to the funeral, when on March 24th the scripture on our Cheering Words calendar was a verse from the book of Ruth, chapter 3 verse 18, where Naomi says to Ruth, 'Wait my daughter, until you find out what happens.' I knew I needed to heed that message and wait, for what, I did not know.

Several times I found myself telling God that I was still waiting. By the 23rd of April, there had been no further contact from Debbie and I thought I should make contact. However, I was somewhat reticent, as I didn't want to be a nuisance. That evening I switched on my mobile phone to call Debbie and immediately a text message came in from her wanting to check the dates of our holiday!

The holiday was a Friday booking and on the Sunday prior to this Debbie telephoned me saying that she still wanted to meet us. She would contact me on Thursday evening to make arrangements and if I didn't hear from her would I please call. Debbie also said that Ron's funeral was to take place a few days after our returning home from holiday in Essex. I knew that I could not return so soon and here was the answer to my question of what to do about attending Ron's funeral. It was quite clear.

Debbie went on to ask, 'Has Uncle John contacted you?' 'No. Why?' I replied. 'Oh, because he asked me for your telephone number and I gave it to him.' I felt buoyed by the information. It seemed that John wanted to make contact.

After Debbie's phone call I felt much more like making preparations and packing for the holiday. I kept my mobile phone on continually, as I didn't know which number Debbie had given to John and of course, I did not want to miss his call.

Monday, Tuesday, Wednesday and then finally Thursday arrived. We travelled to Sarah's to spend the night so that the journey would not be so long the next day. Janet joined us; she had been at a conference in Liverpool the previous few days. Christopher was to arrive early the following morning. It was nearly time to go to bed and there had been no communication from either Debbie or John. Well, Debbie had said to contact her, so I sent a text message to say that we had arrived safely at Sarah's en route to Essex. We all went to bed; some slept, others didn't.

We were all up early on Friday morning only to have Christopher inform us that he had slept in so there would be a delay in our departure. However, this enabled Sarah, Janet and I to enjoy a pre-journey walk on a lovely spring morning. Christopher arrived shortly after our return and after coffee; we loaded up both cars and began our journey to Essex.

After an uneventful journey, we arrived at the barn, which lived up to all our expectations, including the outdoor swimming pool in which three members of the family enjoyed pre-breakfast swims. The barn really was delightful with an enormous kitchen-diner, which we reckoned could nearly hold a ceilidh or at least one good set of Strip the Willow. The barn also provided plenty of room for the family to spread out in and have their own space.

After settling in and having a meal, I said to the family that I would text Debbie but if there was no reply we must just carry on with our holiday, in a semi normal way. By this time, I felt that if I had no contact with John while in Essex I never would.

I sent a text message and shortly afterwards I received a reply from Debbie, asking what our plans were for the next day – would we like to meet for a cuppa and plan our next get-together? I sent a very positive reply and waited for a call from Debbie the following morning. I went to bed in a much more cheerful frame of mind and slept.

Debbie, true to her word, rang early suggesting that we should go into town, find a parking space and then phone for instructions as to where we would meet at 12 noon. Christopher said, 'Mum, we need to leave here no later than 11 o'clock as it will take three quarters of an hour to get there.' 'Okay, I'll be ready,' and I went to the shower.

We were all ready before our allotted departure time. Checking that I had put my mobile phone into my bag, I discovered that a text message had come in. I had left my phone on but had not been near it during the intervening period. Opening the message, I could hardly believe my eyes when I read: 'Good morning Esther I am John…' John's message was that he would very much like to meet me either with Debbie or on our own, what did I think? What did I think! I was overjoyed. The message came through at 9:20am and it was now about 10:15am. We decided that it was probably best to meet John and Debbie together for the first time. It would be an emotional time for them and they were going to be meeting with five of us, so the return message said that we would meet John with Debbie. John's reply said, 'Thank you Esther, see you very soon.' Wow!

Debbie informed us as to where we should meet, also exchanging messages regarding the clothes that both of us would be wearing for easy identification. Debbie was to be wearing a green jacket. I was in pale blue. By this time we were already on our way! It seemed to take forever. I was convinced the satnav was not working properly but eventually we arrived.

We parked and walked to the street where the chosen tearoom was located. Janet disappeared into a shop, quite a usual occurrence, but she did not emerge very quickly. We watched the tearoom for any sign of someone wearing a green jacket but there was no one that we could see. It was now 12 noon and still no sign of Janet. Sarah said, 'Mum, you and Dad go into the tearoom, Debbie may be inside. I'll wait for Christopher and Janet.' Addie went first and as soon as he pushed the door open he said, 'That's John over there,' having recognised him from photos that Ron and Sandra had given us. Debbie's back was to us but John saw us and immediately stood up and it was hugs all round with Debbie, John and his wife Lorna.

I think they got quite a surprise when another three of the Harkess family walked in. Borrowing chairs from other tables the eight of us sat enjoying coffee taking it in turn to introduce ourselves to each other. After about an hour Debbie said that she must go but would be in touch to arrange our next meeting. As it was lunchtime and the café obviously required the table John gave us the choice of having lunch at the café or at John and Lorna's home. We naturally chose the latter.

It was a beautiful day and we were able to sit in John and Lorna's garden soaking up the warm spring sunshine while enjoying a delicious sandwich lunch. I found it so incredible that I was sitting in my brother's garden, eating lunch, with him sat next to me, when only hours before I had despaired of ever meeting him. I was just overflowing with thanks to God for answering my prayers, even if it took a long time. At one point John said, 'You've just laughed like you did in the café.' 'Yes,' I said. He replied, 'It's nearly thirty years since I last heard that laugh.' Could I laugh like somebody that I had never met? I understand that I can look like Grace and have other characteristics but to laugh like her, well, I found that astonishing.

After a while John's daughter Chloe and her boyfriend came to say hello with another round of hugs taking place.

When Chloe walked into the garden Christopher thought he was seeing Sarah's little sister!

We eventually left with plans for John and Lorna to come and have a meal with us one evening. This must go into the category of being one of the most remarkable days of my life.

We went back to the barn, to relax and make plans for the rest of our time in Essex. The good weather continued and we really enjoyed exploring the countryside, which was resplendent in its spring garb, with high hedges of May blossoms in full bloom. The roadside verges were swathed in a sea of cow parsley, which is a favourite of mine. There were many *ooh's* and *ah's* and 'look at that!' as we drove past delightful cottages and houses, with wisteria cascading down the walls.

We went to Ron's home on the Tuesday morning to meet Debbie and Colleen, a friend of Ron's. Colleen told me that she had been with Ron when the letter from Birthlink arrived. Ron read the letter and handed it to her saying. 'What do you make of this?' Handing it back to him she replied, 'I think you have just gone and got another sister.'

Debbie produced many photos for us to look at and every so often, there were exclamations of '*Wow*, so and so looks like so and so at a certain age!' We sat there drinking coffee wondering what Ron would have thought of us all being together without him. However, I was so pleased to visit his home, seeing what I had only been able to imagine until then.

Christopher, knowing that Ron had been going to take me to see the house where Grace had lived with her parents and which we had come across so many times in our search, suggested that we head for Romford. With a satnav to direct us, we set off on another visit into the past.

We found the address without too much trouble and proceeded to take photographs, then retracing our route I took photographs of the church where Grace and Eric were married.

This was lovely, as Debbie had just shown me their wedding photograph that morning.

It was well into the afternoon and certain members of the family were crying out for food! Sarah very wisely suggested that we go to a nearby Sainsbury's supermarket. Once our appetites were sated, we then shopped for food to make a meal for our visitors who were coming the following evening.

The next day we spent a very enjoyable time in Constable Country admiring yet more lovely old buildings, wisteria and of course, the scenery that had so inspired the famous painter.

Once back at the barn we prepared the meal for our guests and awaited their arrival. John and Lorna arrived just after 7pm and there was much family talk as we sat around the meal table. Afterwards as we sat drinking coffee in the sitting room John told me how difficult it had been for him to make contact with me, but he was so pleased that he had finally done so. I reassured him that I really did understand and how happy I was that he had decided to meet me. Ron had told me that making his first telephone call to me was one of the most difficult things he had ever had to do.

Their visit lasted into the wee small hours and we really felt for them, as they then had to drive home and be up early having had little sleep. I did text John later the following day to commiserate with them; he replied, saying the late night had been worth it and he was so glad we had met. That I wholeheartedly agreed with.

What an incredible few days it had been, probably best described as an emotional roller coaster. A holiday, which at the outset I dreaded, was now, completely turned around by the love and acceptance of me and my family by my 'Down South family' in Essex. I returned home hoping that my visit to Essex would not be the last.

Looking back over 70 years there is so much for which I have to be thankful. I can see the amazing plan of my life with all the ups, downs, twists and turns. How the painful times whatever the cause can so often be of benefit.

If it had not been for Mummy, Daddy, Auntie Lah, Addie, Christopher, Janet and Sarah and many others too numerous to mention, my life would have been the poorer.

The fulfilment of those prophetic words written by Grace in 1944, 'I know that God will bless her and keep her in his keeping,' has certainly happened, continuing to this day and into eternity.

Epilogue

GRACE

IF IT HADN'T BEEN for Grace there would have been No Esther, No Ron, No Ian, No John, No Sue, No Sandra.

If it hadn't been for Grace there would have been No Christopher, No Sarah.

If it hadn't been for The Grace of God there would be No assurance of eternal life.

UNENDING LOVE, AMAZING GRACE.

Organisations relevant to the content of this book

Birthlink
21 Castle Street, Edinburgh. EH2 3DN. UK.
Tel. 0131-225-64441

Christian Family Concern
42 South Park Hill Road, South Croydon. CR2 7YB. UK.
Tel. 020-8667-9755

The Faith Mission
548 Gilmerton Road, Gilmerton, Edinburgh. EH17 7JD. UK.
Tel. 0131-64-5814

Scottish Bible Society
7 Hampton Place, Edinburgh. EH12 5XU
Tel. 0131-337-9701